The German-Speaking Countries of Europe

A Selective Bibliography

Margrit B. Krewson

Library of Congress   Washington   1985

Library of Congress Cataloging in Publication Data

Krewson, Margrit B. (Margrit Beran), 1936–
  The German-speaking countries of Europe.

  Includes index.
  1.Europe, German-speaking—Bibliography. I. Title.
Z2000.K73 1985 [D1051]   016.94′00975   85–45168
ISBN 0-8444-0503-5

ju
10-1-86

CONTENTS

INTRODUCTION

This bibliography has been compiled to provide students, researchers, and scholars with a current guide to sources on the German-speaking countries: Austria, the German Democratic Republic, the Federal Republic of Germany, Liechtenstein, and Switzerland.

The following subject areas have been selected:

Bibliographies and Reference Works
Description and Travel
Economy
Intellectual and Cultural Life
Politics and Government
Religion
Society

The items selected have been chosen on the basis of their date of publication. Available bibliographies stop with the 1970s. This one emphasizes the 1980s, with excursions into the 1970s when no later title on the same subject is available. We also focused on the broad nature of their appeal within their subject area, and their availability to the reading public. All items cited can be found in the collections of the Library of Congress. Preference has been given to English-language sources. Where no comparable English sources were available, German-language sources have been cited.

Despite common ties of language and culture, the nations represented are diverse and individual in nature. The sources selected, though weighted in favor of the more populous states, attempt to highlight the uniqueness of these countries and to present a representative sampling of opinion and subject orientation. Special attention has been given to the interaction between the German-speaking countries and the United States. This is particularly true under the subject headings of economy and politics and government. This emphasis emerges from the assumption that American researchers will be more concerned with the relationship of these countries to the United States then with purely domestic developments within the German-speaking countries.

I wish to thank David H. Kraus, Acting Chief of the European Division, for his assistance during all stages of this project, and Mrs. Helen E. Saunders, who saw this text through its various drafts and final preparation for publication.

Margrit B. Krewson

May 1985

AUSTRIA

Bibliographies and Reference Works

1

Breu, Josef. Geographisches Namenbuch Österreichs = Gazetteer of Austria. Wien: Verl. d. Österr. Akad. d. Wiss., 1975. xiv, 323 p. (Forschungen zur theoretischen Kartographie; Bd. 3)   DB14.B73

"Österreichische Akademie der Wissenschaften. Veröffentlichungen des Instituts für Kartographie." Introd. material also in English.

2

GOF-Verlag, Vienna. GOF-Ortsverzeichnis von Österreich für Wirtschaft und Verkehr. 9. Aufl., neu bearb., erw. u. verb. durch die Aufnahme weiterer Orte, d. Berücks. aller Gemeindeveränderungen, Auflassung v. Bezirksgerichten etc., sowie durch die Intensivierung d. Entfernungsangaben d. Orte zum jeweiligen Bahnhof. Wien: GOF-Verl., 1978. 394 p.   HE3054.G2 1978

3

Low, Alfred D. The Anschluss movement, 1918–1938: Background and aftermath: an annotated bibliography of German and Austrian nationalism. New York: Garland, 1984. xix, 186 p. (Canadian review of studies in nationalism; vol. 4)   Z2120.L68 1984
Includes index.

4

Malina, Peter. Bibliographie zur österreichischen Zeitgeschichte 1918–1978: eine Auswahl. Wien: Verl. f. Geschichte u. Politik, 1978. 70 p. (Politische Bildung; Heft 28–30)   Z2120.3.M34
Includes index.

5

Oberschelp, Reinhard. Die Bibliographien zur deutschen Landesgeschichte und Landeskunde. 2., völlig neu bearb. Aufl. Frankfurt am Main: Klostermann, 1977. 106 p. (Zeitschrift für Bibliothekswesen und Bibliographie: Sonderheft; 7)   Z2243.O25 1977
Includes index.
Bibliography: 49–98.

6

Paulhart, Herbert. Österreichische historische Bibliographie: Liste der Zeitschriften 1945-1979 = Austrian historical bibliography; list of periodicals 1945-1979. Salzburg: W. Neugebauer; Santa Barbara, Cal.: Clio Press, 1980. 32 p. (Österreichische historische Bibliographie. Beiheft; 1 = Austrian historical bibliography. Supplement; 1)

Z2120.3.P38 1980

Includes index.

7

Schmidt, Leopold, 1912- Gegenwartsvolkskunde: eine bibliogr. Einführung. Wien: Verl. d. Österr. Akad. d. Wiss., 1976. 153 p. (Mitteilungen des Instituts für Gegenwartsvolkskunde: Sonderband; 1)

Z5117.S35

Includes index.

8

Schubert, Peter. Schauplatz Österreich: topographisches Lexikon zur Zeitgeschichte in drei Bänden. Wien: Brüder Hollinek, 1976-1980. 3 v.

DB15.S38

Includes indexes.
Bibliography: v. 1, p. 311-313.
Contents.—Bd. 1. Wien. Bd. 2.
Bundesländerorte A-K. Bd. 3.
Bundesländerorte L-Z.

9

Senekovic, Dagmar. Handy guide to Austrian genealogical records. Logan, Utah: Everton Publishers, 1979. 97 p.: maps.   CS504.S46

10

Spalek, John M. Guide to the archival materials of the German-speaking emigration to the United States after 1933 = Verzeichnis der Quellen und Materialien der deutschsprachigen Emigration in den U.S.A. seit 1933. Charlottesville: Published for the Bibliographical Society of the University of Virginia by the University Press of Virginia, 1978. xxv, 1133 p.   Z6611.G46S62

Includes indexes.

11

Stock, Karl Franz. Bibliographie österreichischer Bibliographien, Sammelbiographien und Nachschlagewerke. Graz, Wienerstrasse 260: K. F. Stock [Selbstverlag], 1978. 302 p., v. 4, pt. 1.

Z2101.A1S86 v. 4, pt. 1

Includes index.

12

Wernigg, Ferdinand. Bibliographie österreichischer Drucke während der
"erweiterten Pressfreiheit" 1781-1795: [Zsgest. auf Grundlage d.
Bestände d. Wiener Stadtbibliothek u. des Katalogs d. Univer-
sitätsbibliothek Wien, ergänzt durch zeitgenössische Bibliographien].
Wien; München: Jugend und Volk, 1973-1979. 2 v. (Veröf-
fentlichungen aus der Wiener Stadtbibliothek; Folge 4, 6) (Wiener
Schriften; Heft 35, 41)   Z674.V52a Folge 4, 6
Includes indexes.
Bibliography: v. 1, p. 429.

Description and Travel

13

Evans, Craig, 1949- On foot through Europe: a trail guide to Austria,
Switzerland & Liechtenstein. New York: Quill,1982. xv, 211 p.: maps.
GV199.44A9E9 1982
Includes bibliographical references.

14

Das Grosse farbige Österreichbuch: Austria = Autriche. Wien;
Heidelberg: Ueberreuter, 1980. 111 p.: chiefly ill. (all col.).
DB19.G73
English, French, and German.

15

Harrison, John. Austria & Switzerland. Chicago: Rand McNally, 1983.
128 p.: col. ill.   DB16.H3 1983
Includes index.

16

Langthaler, Gerhart. Das andere Österreich: die reale Perspektive =
L'autre Autriche: la perspective réelle = The other Austria: the real
perspective. Wien: Molden, 1981. 203 p.: 312 col. ill.
DB19.L34 1981
Parallel text in English, French, and German.

17

Niel, Alfred. Die k.u.k. Riviera: von Abbazia bis Grado. Graz; Wien;
Köln: Styria, 1981. 120 p.: 101 ill.   DR1350.A35N53 1981
Includes indexes.
Bibliography: p. 120.

18
Schmitt, Hilmar, 1936– Österreich: Schlösser, Burgen, Klöster. München: Ringier, 1981. 224 p.: ill. (some col.); Col. ill. on lining papers.

DB27.5.S35 1981

Includes indexes.
Bibliography: p. 224.

19
Siegert, Heinz, 1924– Das grosse Österreich-Reisebuch: Ratgeber-Atlas f. Urlaub u. Freizeit. Berlin; Stuttgart: Reise- und Verkehrsverl., 1975. 286 p.: numerous col. ill., maps.

DB16.S53

Legends also in English and French.
Includes index.
Bibliography: p. 287.

Economy

20
Die Amtliche Statistik in Österreich, gestern, heute, morgen: ausgewählte Ergebnisse und Probleme/bearb. im Österreichischen Statistischen Zentralamt. Wien: Das Amt: Kommissionsverlag C. Ueberreuter, 1978. 266 p. (Beiträge zur österreichischen Statistik; Heft 483)

HA1173.A27 Heft 483

21
Arbeitskreis für Ökonomische und Soziologische Studien. Wachstumsalternativen: strukturelle Konsequenzen einer längerfristigen Wachstumsabschwächung. Wien: Wirtschaftsverl. Orac, 1980. 70 p.

HC265.A765 1980

Includes bibliographical references.

22
Bobek, Hans, 1903– Gliederung Österreichs in wirtschaftliche Strukturgebiete. Wien: Verlag der Österreichischen Akademie der Wissenschaften, 1981. xii, 113 p.: ill., col. maps. (Beiträge zur Regionalforschung; Bd. 3)

HC265.B582 1981

Three maps and 21 tables on folded leaves in pocket.
Includes bibliographical references.

23
Butschek, Felix. Vollbeschäftigung in der Krise: die österreichische Erfahrung 1974 bis 1979. Wien: Wirtschaftsverlag Orac, 1981. 130 p ill.

HD5771.B87 1981

Bibliography: p. 127–130.

24

Faber, Malte Michael. Introduction to modern Austrian capital theory. Berlin; New York: Springer-Verlag, 1979. x, 196 p.; ill. (Lecture notes in economics and mathematical systems; 167: Mathematical economics)

Includes indexes.
Bibliography: p. 181-191

HB501.F22

25

Findl, Peter. Die Bevölkerung Österreichs: demographische Strukturen u. Trends: aus Anlass des Weltbevölkerungsjahres 1974 d. Vereinten Nationen verf. im Österr. Statist. Zentralamt. Wien: Österr. Staatsdruckerei in Komm., 1977. 169 p.: ill. (Beiträge zur österreichischen Statistik; 463. Heft)   HA1173.A27 Heft 463
Bibliography: p. 167-169.

26

Handschur, Peter. Analyse des österreichischen Agraraussenhandels 1966-1978 = Austrian foreign trade of agricultural commodities 1966-1978. Wien: Österr. Agrarverl., 1979. 122 p.: graphs. (Schriftenreihe des Agrarwirtschaftlichen Institutes des Bundesministeriums für Land- und Forstwirtschaft; Nr. 29).   HD9015.A8H36
Summary also in English.
Includes bibliographical references.

27

Hankel, Wilhelm, 1919– Prosperität in der Krise: eine Analyse d. Wirtschaftspolitik in d. Energiekrise am Beispiel Österreichs: aktive Binnenbilanz durch passive Aussenbilanz. Wien; München; Zürich; Innsbruck: Molden, 1979. 228 p.: ill.   HC265.H32
Includes bibliographical references.

28

Höll, Otmar. Austria's technological dependence: basic dimensions and current trends. Laxenburg, Austria: Austrian Institute for International Affairs, 1980. i, 63 p.: ill. (The Laxenburg papers; no. 2).

HC270.T4H64 1980
Bibliography: p. 60-63.

29

Hutchison, T. W. (Terence Wilmot) The politics and philosophy of economics: Marxians, Keynesians, and Austrians. New York: New York University Press, 1981. x, 310 p.   HB75.H792
Includes bibliographies and index.

30

Kager, Marianne. Entwicklung der Industriestruktur in Österreich und der BRD 1960-1975. Wien: Orac, 1979. 246 p. (Schriftenreihe des Ludwig-Boltzmann-Institutes für Wachstumsforschung; Bd. 4)
Bibliography: p. 240-243.
HC265.K275

31

Kausel, Anton. Die österreichische Wirtschaft ist kerngesund: Beurteilung d. nachhaltigen Wettbewerbsstärke d. österr. Wirtschaft auf Grund makroökonomischer Tatbestände. Wien: Bundesmin. f. Finanzen, 1979. 52 p.: graphs.   HC265.K378

32

Längerfristige Aspekte der Engergieversorgung/Beirat für Wirtschafts- und Sozialfragen. Wien.: Kommissionsverlag, C. Ueberreuter, 1982. 128 p.   HD9502.A92L36 1982
Includes bibliographcal references.

33

Littlechild, S. C. The fallacy of the mixed economy: an ''Austrian'' critique of conventional economics and government policy. San Francisco, Calif.: Cato Institute, 1979. xiv, 85 p.   HB98.L58 1979
Bibliography: p. 81-83.

34

März, Eduard. Österreichische Bankpolitik in der Zeit der grossen Wende 1913-1923: am Beispiel der Creditanstalt für Handel und Gewerbe. München: Oldenbourg: Wien: Verlag für Geschichte und Politik, 1981. 608 p., [8] p. of plates: ill.   HG3020.V54O475 1981
Includes index.
Bibliography: p. 590-604.

35

Management der achtziger Jahre: Perspektiven einer Herausforderung/herausgegeben von Eduard Mayer. Wien: Multiplex Media Verlag, 1980. 336 p.: ill.   HD70.A8M36 1980
Includes bibliographical references.

36

New directions in Austrian economics/edited by Louis M. Spadaro. Kansas City [Kan.]: Sheed Andrews and McMeel, 1978. x, 239 p.: ill. (Studies in economic theory).   HB98.N48

Papers presented at a symposium sponsored by the University College at Buckingham and the Institute for Humane Studies, and held at Windsor Castle Sept. 1976.
Includes bibliographical references and index.

37

Österreichisches Institut für Raumplanung. Extrapolation der Bevölkerungsentwicklung bis zum Jahr 1991 in den Stadt- und Wohnungsmarktregionen. Wien: ÖIR, 1975. 253 p. in various pagings. HB3591.O46 1975
Includes bibliographical references.

38

The Political economy of Austria/edited by Sven W. Arndt. Washington, D. C.: American Enterprise Institute for Public Policy Research, 1982. xiv, 224 p.: ill HC265.P64 1982
Proceedings of a conference in the early autumn of 1981 sponsored by the Austrian Institute in New York and the American Enterprise Institute.
Includes bibliographical references.

39

Volkszählung 1981/bearbeitet im Österreichischen Statistischen Zentralamt. Wien: Das Amt, 1982. 83 p. HA1173.A27 Heft 630/1
(Beiträge zur österreichischen Statistik; 630/1. Heft-).

40

Wölfling, Manfred. Die Industriestruktur in Österreich und in der DDR: eine komparativempirische Studie. Wien: Wiener Institut für Internationale Wirtschaftsvergleiche, 1980. 31 p.
(Forschungsberichte/Wiener Institut für Internationale Wirtschaftsvergleiche; Nr. 63) HC265.W575 1980
Includes bibliographical references.

Intellectual and Cultural Life

41

Aufbruch und Untergang: österreichische Kultur zwischen 1918 und 1938/Franz Kadrnoska (Hrsg.); mit einem Vorwort von Hertha Firnberg. Wien: Europaverlag. 1981. 640 p.: ill. DB97.A93 1981
Includes bibliographies and index.

42

Austria, its people and culture/William O. Westervelt, editor-in-chief.
Skokie, IL: National Textbook Co., 1980. 94 p.: ill.

DB30.A79 1980

43

Brix, Emil. Die Umgangssprachen in Altösterreich zwischen Agitation
und Assimilation: die Sprachenstatistik in den zisleithanischen
Volkszählungen, 1880 bis 1910. Wien: Böhlau, 1982. 537 p., [1] leaf
of plates: ill.   HA1184.B74 1982
(Veröffentlichungen der Kommission für Neuere Geschichte Österreichs; Bd. 72) Originally presented as the author's thesis (doctoral—
Universität Wien, 1979), under the title: Die nationale Frage anhand
der Umgangssprachenerhebungen in den zisleithanischen Volkszählungen, 1880 bis 1910.
Includes index.
Bibliography: p. 508–524.

44

Brucher, Günter. Barockarchitekur in Österreich. Köln: DuMont, 1983.
360 p.: ill. (some col.).   NA1006.B78 1983
Includes bibliographical references and indexes.

45

Dawid, Maria. Österreich, Kunstschätze. Innsbruck: Pinguin Verl.,
Frankfurt/M.: Umschau Verl., 1977. 200 p.: chiefly col. ill.
N6801.D35
Bibliography: p. 192.

46

Gabriel, Norbert, 1957– Peter Handke und Österreich. Bonn: Bouvier,
1983. 265 p.   PT2668.A5Z64 1983
Bibliography: p. 257-265.
(Abhandlungen zur Kunst-, Musik- und Literaturwissenschaft; Bd.
334)

47

Galántai, József. Die Österreichisch-Ungarische Monarchie und der
Weltkrieg. [Budapest]: Corvina, 1979. 406 p., [7] leaves of plates: ill.
DR38.3.A9G3415
Bibliography: p. 386–388.

48

Gardos, Harald. Some aspects of cultural policies in Austria. Paris:
Unesco, 1981. 71 p., [4] p. of plates: ill.   DB99.2.G37
Includes bibliographical references.

49

Das Grössere Österreich: geistiges und soziales Leben von 1880 bis zur Gegenwart: hundert Kapitel mit einem Essay von Ernst Krenek, Von der Aufgabe, ein Österreicher zu sein/herausgegeben von Kristian Sotriffer. Wien: Edition Tusch. 1982. 550 p.: ill. (some col.).

DB30.G76 1982

Includes index.
Bibliography: p. 538.

50

Grunfeld, Fredric V. Prophets without honour: a background to Freud, Kafka, Einstein, and their world. New York: McGraw-Hill, 1980. xi, 347 p.: ports. DS135.G33G8 1980
Includes index.
Bibliography: p. 323-334.

51

Johnston, William M., 1936- The Austrian mind; an intellectual and social history, 1848-1938. Berkeley, University of California Press, 1972. xv, 515 p. illus. DB30.J64
Bibliography: p. 475-494.

52

Johnston, William M., 1936- Vienna, Vienna, English. Vienna, Vienna: the golden age, 1815-1914. New York: C. N. Potter: Distributed by Crown Publishers, 1981. 332 p.: ill. (some col.).

DB854.J6413 1981

Translated from Italian.
Includes index.
Bibliography: p. 328.

53

Keil-Budischowsky, Verena, 1941- Die Theater Wiens. Wien: P. Zsolnay. 1983. 410 p.: 132 ill. PN2616.V5K44 1983
Includes bibliographical references.
(Wiener Geschichtsbücher; Bd. 30/31/32).

54

Knaurs Kulturführer in Farbe Österreich [Hrsg., Franz N. Mehling; Autoren, Marianne Mehling . . . et al.]. München; Zürich: Droemer-Knaur, 1977. 560 p.: numerous col. ill., maps. N6801.K57
Includes index.

55

Köstler, Gisela. Geheimnis und Zauber im Alpenland: Aberglaube im
bäuerlichen Jahrlauf. Graz; Wien; Köln: Verl. Styria, 1980. 213 p.: ill.
GR159.A43K63

56

Modern Austria/editor, Kurt Steiner. Palo Alto, Calif.: Society for the
Promotion of Science and Scholarship, 1981. xxvi, 527 p.: ill.
DB17.M63 1981
Includes bibliographies and index.

57

Schindler, Herbert, 1923– Kunstreisen in Österreich: von Passau nach
Wien. München: Prestel, 1982. 520 p., [1] folded leaf of plates: ill.
(some col.). N6801.S42 1982
Includes index.

58

Schorske, Carl E. Fin-de-siècle Vienna: politics and culture. New York:
Vintage Books, 1981. xxx, 378 p., [8] leaves of plates: ill.
DB851.S42 1981
Includes bibliographical references and index.

59

Vienna. Österreichische Galerie. Die uns verliessen: österreichische Maler
und Bildhauer der Emigration und Verfolgung: [Ausstellung, Österreichische Galerie im Oberen Belvedere in Wien, 28. Mai bis 27. Juli
1980. Wien: im Selbstverlag der Österreichischen Galerie, 1980.
215 p.: numerous ill. N1708.A54 nr. 95
Includes bibliographical references.

60

Wagner, Renate. Würde, Glanz und Freude: vom festlichen Leben und
Treiben in den Zeiten. Graz; Wien; Köln: Styria-Verlag. Edition
Kaleidoskop, 1981. 239 p.: 190 ill. (some col.).
GT4848.A2W3 1981
Bibliography: p. 238–239.

Politics and Government

61

Aebi, Alfred. Der Beitrag neutraler Staaten zur Friedenssicherung: untersucht am Beispiel Österreichs und der Schweiz. Zürich: Schweizerischer

Aufklärungs-Dienst;Stäfa: Auslfg. im Buchh.
Th. Guf, 1976. xvi, 236 p. (Schriften des Schweizerischen
Aufklärungs-Dienstes; 14)   UA670.A35 1976
Originally presented as the author's thesis, 4 Geneva.
Includes indexes.
Bibliography: p. 205–229.

62

Die Ära Kreisky: Schwerpunkte der österreichischen Aussenpolitik/
Heraugegeben von Erich Bielka, Peter Jankowitsch, Hans Thalberg.
Wien: Europaverlag, 1983. 351 p.   DB99.2.A45 1983
Includes index.

63

Andics, Hellmut. Die Insel der Seligen: Österreich von der Moskauer
Deklaration bis zur Gegenwart. Wien; München: Molden-
Taschenbuch-Verlag, 1976. 366 p., [16] leaves of plates: ill. (His Öster-
reich 1804–1975; 4)   DB80.A49 Bd. 4
Includes bibliographical references and index.

64

Andics, Hellmut. Das österreichische Jahrhundert: die Donaumonarchie
v. 1804 bis 1900. Bearb. u. erw. Ausg. Wien; München: MTV,
Molden-Taschenbuch-Verl., Eroica Verlagsges., 1976. 317 p.: ill. (His
Österreich 1804–1975; Bd. 1).   DB80.A49 Bd. 1
Includes bibliographical references and index.

65

Andics, Hellmut. Der Staat, den keiner wollte: Österreich von der Grün-
dung der Republik bis zur Moskauer Deklaration. Wien; München:
Molden-Taschenbuch-Verlag, 1976. 363 p., [16] leaves of plates: ill.
(His Österreich 1804–1975; 3).   DB80.A49 Bd. 3
Includes bibliographical references and index.

66

Aretin, Karl Otmar, Freiherr von, 1923– Vom Deutschen Reich zum
Deutschen Bund. Göttingen: Vandenhoeck und Ruprecht, 1980.
213 p. (Deutsche Geschichte; Bd. 7)   DD193.A7
Includes index.
Bibliography: p. 188–193.

67

The Austrian solution—international conflict and cooperation. Charlottesville: Published for the Johns Hopkins Foreign Policy Institute,

School of Advanced International Studies, the Johns Hopkins University by the University Press of Virginia, 1982. xvii, 217 p.

DB99.2.A83 1982

Includes bibliographical references.

68

Barker, Thomas Mack. The Slovene minority of Carinthia. New York: Columbia University Press, 1979.   DB290.7.B3 1979
Includes index.

69

Brauneder, Wilhelm, 1943– Österreichische Verfassungsgeschichte. 2., erg. Aufl. Wien: Manz, 1980. 288 p.: ill. (some col.).

JN1611.B7 1980

Includes bibliographical references and index.

70

Carsten, Francis Ludwig. Faschismus in Österreich: von Schönerer zu Hitler. München: W. Fink, 1978. 373 p. (Kritische Information; 55)

DB86.C3515 1978

Includes index.
Bibliography: p. 351–358.

71

Deutschland und Österreich/hrsg. von Robert A. Kann und Friedrich E. Prinz. Wien; München: Jugend und Volk, 1980. 596 p.: ill., maps (some col.). (Ein Bilaterales Geschichtsbuch)   DD120.A8D48
Includes indexes.
Bibliography: p. 521–560.

72

Eberwein, Wolf-Dieter, 1943– The adaptation of foreign ministries to structural changes in the international system: a comparative study of the Ministries for Foreign Affairs of Austria and the FRG. Laxenburg: Austrian Institute for International Affairs, 1981. v, 75 p. (The Laxenburg papers; no. 3).   JX1687.E32 1981
Bibliography: p. 72–75.

73

Eger, Reiner. Krisen an Österreichs Grenzen: das Verhalten Österreichs während des Ungarnaufstandes 1956 und der tschechoslowakischen Krise 1968: ein Vergleich. Wien: Herold, 1981. 223 p.

DB99.2.E35 1981

Includes documents.
Bibliography: p. 171–188.

74

Friedrichsmeier, Helmut, 1944– 1999: Staatsbürger, Verwaltung, Verfassung: eine Prognose. Wien; München: Jugend & Volk, 1979. 293 p.: ill.   JN2012.3.F74
    Includes bibliographical references.

75

Fussenegger, Gertrud, 1912– Maria Theresia. Mit 33 Schwarzweissabb, u. 3 Kt. Wien; München; Zürich; Innsbruck: Molden, 1980. 312 p.: ill., maps.   DB71.F87

76

Gauss, Adalbert Karl. Wege und Irrwege in Rot-Weiss-Rot: Zeitgeschichtliches u. Interviews mit Bundeskanzler Dr. Kreisky . . . [et al.]. Salzburg: Österr. Flüchtlingsarchiv (ÖFA), Donauschwäb. Kulturzentrum, Haus d. Donauschwaben, 1979. 180 p.: ill., ports. (Donauschwäbische Beiträge; Bd. 73)   JV7843.G38
    Includes bibliographical references.

77

Gerlich, Peter. Staatsbürger und Volksvertretung: das Alltagsverständnis von Parlament und Demokratie in Österreich. Salzburg: Neugebauer, 1981. 267 p.: ill.   JN2026.G47 1981
    Includes index.
    Bibliography: p. 259–263.

78

Gerlich, Rudolf. Die gescheiterte Alternative: Sozialisierung in Österreich nach dem Ersten Weltkrieg. Wien: Braumüller, 1980. xi, 525 p.   DB97.G47 1980
    A revision of the author's thesis. Vienna, 1975.
    Bibliography: p. 361–376.

79

Goldner, Franz, 1903– Austrian emigration, 1938-1945. New York: F. Ungar Pub. Co., 1979. xii, 212 p.   DB34.5.G6513 1979
    Translation of The 2d ed. of Die österreichische Emigration, 1938-1945.
    Includes index.
    Bibliography: p. 169–171.

80

Goldner, Franz, 1903– Dollfuss im Spiegel der US-Akten: aus den Archiven des Secretary of State, Washington, bisher unveröffentlichte

Berichte d. US-Botschaften Wien, Berlin, Rom, London, Paris, Prag.
St. Pölten: Verl. Niederösterr. Pressehaus, 1979. 168 p.
DB98.D6G62
Includes texts in English.
Includes index.
Bibliography: p. 163–166.

81
Hajek, Helmut. Der Wandel des Krankheitenspektrums in Österreich seit der Jahrhundertwende. Wien: Österr. Bundesinst. f. Gesundheitswesen, 1979.180, [76] p.   RA493.H34
"Im Auftrag des Bundesministeriums für Gesundheit und Umweltsschutz."
Includes bibliographical references.

82
Hankel, Wilhelm, 1929– Prosperity amidst crisis: Austria's economic policy and the energy crunch. Boulder, Colo.: Westview Press, 1981.
xxii, 234 p.: ill.   HC265.H3213
Includes bibliographical references and index.

83
Kaindl, Franz, 1932– Orden und Ehrenzeichen: Katalog zur Sonderausstellung. Wien: Heeresgeschichtl. Museum, 1976. 54 p., [4] leaves of plates: ill.   UB435.A9K34
Includes index.
Bibliography: p. 48–51.

84
Katzenstein, Peter J. Disjoined partners: Austria and Germany since 1815. Berkeley: University of California Press, 1976. xv, 263 p.: ill.
JX1547.Z7G475
Includes bibliographical references and index.

85
Kienesberger, Peter. Sie nannten uns Terroristen. Freiheitskampf in Südtirol. Wien, Südtirol-Informations-Zentrum (1971). 392 p.
DG975.B68K54
"Sonderband der Schriftenreihe des Südtirol-Informations-Zentrums der Volksbewegung für Südtirol."

86
Kreisky, Bruno. Politik braucht Visionen: Aufsätze, Reden und Interviews zu aktuellen weltpolitischen Fragen. Königstein/Ts.: Athenäum,

1982. xii, 240 p. DB98.K7A25 1982
Bibliography of the author's works: p. 238.

87

Kreisky, Eva. Alternative Strategien der Organisationen staatlichen Handelns: Begleitstudie zum OECD-Project "Integrierte Gesellschafts-politik": Endbericht. Wien: Inst. f. Höhere Studien, 1979. 317 p., [8] p. JN2012.3.K73
"Im Auftrag des Bundeskanzleramtes."
Bibliography: p. 319-325.

88

Low, Alfred D. The Anschluss movement, 1918-1938: background and aftermath: an annotated bibliography of German and Austrian nationalism. New York: Garland, 1984. xix, 186 p.
(Canadian review of studies in nationalism; vol. 4)
Z2120.L68 1984
Includes index.

89

Maass, Walter B. Country without a name: Austria under Nazi rule, 1938-1945. New York: F. Ungar Pub. Co., 1979. x, 178 p.: ill.
DB99.M3
Includes index.
Bibliography: p. 165-167.

90

Maleta, Alfred. Bewältigte Vergangenheit: Österreich 1932-1945. Graz; Wien; Köln: Verlag Styria, 1981. 250 p. DB96.M32
Includes index.

91

Matsch, Erwin. Geschichte des Auswärtigen Dienstes von Österreich (-Ungarn), 1720-1920. Wien; Köln; Graz: Böhlau, 1980. 203 p., [6] p. of plates: ports. JX1792.A4 1980
Includes bibliographical references and index.

92

Mraz, Gerda. Maria Theresia: ihr Leben u. ihre Zeit in Bildern u. Dokumenten. München: Süddeutscher Verlag, 1979. 363 p.: 455 ill. (some col.), maps (some col.). DB71.M78
Includes index.
Bibliography: p. 338-343.

93

Österreich zur See. Wien: Österr. Bundesverl., 1980. 191 p. (Schriften des Heeresgeschichtl. Museums in Wien) (Militärwissenschaftliches Institut; Bd. 8).   U13.V6H45 Bd. 8
Summaries in English.
Includes indexes.
Bibliography: p. 112-164.

94

Pauley, Bruce F. Hitler and the forgotten Nazis: a history of Austrian national socialism. Chapel Hill: University of North Carolina Press, 1981. xxi, 292 p.: ill.   DB97.P38
Includes index.
Bibliography: p. 267-282.

95

Pelinka, Anton, 1941- Modellfall Österreich?: Möglichkeiten und Grenzen der Sozialpartnerschaft. Wien: Braumüller, 1981. vii, 117 p.: ill. (Studien zur österreichischen und internationalen Politik; Bd. 4)
JN2016.P7P44 1981
Includes bibliographical references and index.

96

Piringer, Kurt. Die Geschichte der Freiheitlichen: Beitrag der dritten Kraft zur österreichischen Politik. Wien: Orac; [Stuttgart]: Pietsch, 1982. 343 p.: ill.   JN1999.F7P57 1982
Includes bibliographical references and index.

97

Plasser, Fritz, 1948- Unbehagen im Parteienstaat: Jugend und Politik in Österreich. Wien: Böhlau, 1982. 208 p.: ill. (Studien zu Politik und Verwaltung; Bd. 2)   JN2030.P57 1982
Bibliography: p. 189-208.

98

Politisches Handbuch Österreichs 1945-1980/zusammengestellt von Wolfgang E. Oberleitner. Abgeschlossen am 20. Jänner 1981. Wien: Österreichischer Bundesverlag, 1981. 287 p.   JN2017.P64 1981
Includes index.

99

Rabinbach, Anson. The crisis of Austrian socialism: from Red Vienna to civil war, 1927-1934. Chicago: University of Chicago Press, 1983.

viii, 296 p., [4] p. of plates: ill.   HX253.R3 1983
Includes index.
Bibliography: p. 263-284.

100

Rauchensteiner, Manfried. Spätherbst 1956: die Neutralität auf dem
Prüfstand. Wien: Österreichischer Bundesverlag, 1981. 123 p., ill.
(some col.); (Eine Veröffentlichung des Heeresgeschichtl. Museums)
                                         DB99.2.R37 1981
Bibliography: p. 122-123.

101

Ritschel, Karl Heinz. Österreich ist frei!:der Weg zum Staatsvertrag 1945
bis 1955. Wien: Edition Tusch, 1980. 229 p.: ill. (some col.).
                                         DB99.1.R57
Bibliography: p. 83.

102

Sully, Melanie A. Political parties and elections in Austria. New York:
St. Martin's Press, 1981. xiii, 194 p.: ill.   JN2030.S85 1981
Includes index.
Bibliography: p.181-184.

103

Toscano, Mario. Alto Adige, South Tyrol: Italy's frontier with the German world. Baltimore: Johns Hopkins University Press. 1975. xii,
283 p.: map.   DG975.T792T6713
Translation of Storia diplomatica della questione dell'Alto Adige.
Includes bibliographical references and index.

104

U. S. occupation in Europe after World War II: papers and reminiscences
from the April 23-24, 1976 conference held at the George C. Mar-
shall Research Foundation, Lexington, Virginia. Lawrence: Regents
Press of Kansas, 1978. viii, 172 p.: maps.   DD257.U54
"A George C. Marshall Research Foundation publication.
Includes bibliographical references and index.

105

Vienna. Dokumentationsarchiv des Österreichischen Widerstandes.
Periodica 1933-1945. Wien: Das Dokumentationsarchiv, 1975. [12],
132 p. [6] leaves of plates: ill. (Katalog—Dokumentationsarchiv des
Österreichischen Widerstandes; Nr. 9)   DB99.V492a Nr. 9.
Includes index.
Bibliography: p. 129-132.

106

Die Wahlen in den Bundesländern seit 1945: Nationalrat und Land-
tage/Herausgeber, Verbindungsstelle der Bundesländer beim Amt der
Niederösterreichischen Landesregierung. 5. erw. Aufl. Wien: Die Verbindungsstelle, 1981. 112 p.: ill. (some col.).

JN2029.5.W33 1981

107

Wistrich, Robert S.,1945- Socialism and the Jews; the dilemmas of
assimilation in Germany and Austria-Hungary. Rutherford, N. J.:
Fairleigh Dickinson University Press; London; East Brunswick, N. J.:
Associated University Presses, 1982. 435 p.

DS135.G33W53 1982

Includes index.
Bibliography: p. 405-427.

Religion

108

Läpple, Alfred, 1915- Kirche und Nationalsozialismus in Deutschland
und Österreich: Fakten, Dokumente, Analysen. Aschaffenburg: Patt-
loch, 1980. 450 p.: ill.   BR856.L32
Includes bibliographical references and index.

109

Power, Michael. Religion in the Reich. New York: AMS Press, 1982.
viii, 240 p. Reprint. Originally published: London; New York:
Longmans, Green, 1939.

BR856.P65 1982

Includes bibliographical references.

110

Siegfried, Klaus-Jörg, 1940- Klerikalfaschismus: zur Entstehung u.
sozialen Funktion d. Dollfussregimes in Österreich: ein Beitr. zur
Faschismusdiskussion. Frankfurt a.M.; Bern; Cirencester/U.K.: Lang,
1979. 132 p. (Sozialwissenschaftliche Studien; Bd. 2)

DB96.S5

Bibliography: p. 121-132.

111

Steger, Gerhard, 1957- Der Brückenschlag: katholische Kirche und
Sozialdemokratie in Österreich. Wien: Jugend und Volk. 1982. 368 p.

DB96.S68 1982

Includes index.
Bibliography: p. 354-358.

Society

112

Durchbruch in die Moderne: von der industriellen zur nachindustriellen Gesellschaft/herausgegeben von Alois Mock; Redaktion Wendelin Ettmayer. Graz; Wien; Köln: Styria, 1981. 347 p.

HN405.5.D87 1981

"Festschrift aus Anlass des 70. Geburtstages von Altbundeskanzler Dr. Josef Klaus"
Includes bibliographical references.

113

Geschichte und Ergebnisse der zentralen amtlichen Statistik in Österreich 1829–1979: Festschrift aus Anlass des 150jähr. Bestehens d. zentralen amtl. Statistik in Österreich/bearb. im Österr. Statist. Zentralamt. Wien: Österr. Staatsdruckerei in Komm., 1979. 720 p.: ill., ports. (Beiträge zur österreichischen Statistik; Heft 550)

HA1173.A27 Heft 550

Includes bibliographical references.

114

Heer, Friedrich, 1916– Der Kampf um die österreichische Identität. Wien; Köln; Graz: Böhlau, 1981. 562 p.   DB38.H43
Includes index.
Bibliography: p. 519–543.

115

Helczmanovszki, Heimold. Mann und Frau in Österreich: ein demographischer Überblick anlässlich des "Jahres d. Frau." Wien: Verl. f. Geschichte u. Politik, 1975. 31 p. (Politische Bildung: Heft 20)

HB3591.H45

116

Integrated social policy: a review of the Austrian experience. Paris: Organization for Economic Co-operation and Development; [Washington, D. C.: Sold by OECD Publications and Information Center], 1981. 257 p.   HN405.5.I57 1981
Includes bibliographies.

117

Kisser, Peter, 1928– 7000 Jahre Vergangenheit: unverwüstliches Österreich. Wien: Zsolnay, 1981. 294, [1] p., [8] p. of plates: ill.

DB38.K57 1981

Bibliography: p. 291–295.

118

Komlos, John, 1944– The Habsburg monarchy as a customs union: economic development in Austria-Hungary in the nineteenth century. Princeton, N. J., Princeton University Press, 1983. xix, 347 p.: ill.

HC265.K59 1983

Rev. version of thesis (Ph.D.)—University of Chicago, 1978.
Includes index.
Bibliography: p. 323–337.

119

Lebensverhältnisse in Österreich; Klassen u. Schichten im Sozialstaat: [e. Projekt d. Inst. für Höhere Studien u. Wissenschaftl. Forschung, Wien/im Auftr. d. Bundesministeriums für Wiss. u. Forschung. Frankfurt/Main; New York: Campus-Verlag, 1980. v, 530 p.

HN420.S6L42

Bibliography: p. 494–517.

120

Luza, Radomir. The resistance in Austria, 1938–1945. Minneapolis: University of Minnesota Press, 1984. xv, 366 p.

D802.A9L89 1984

Includes index.
Bibliography: p. 325–341.

121

So leben wir morgen: Österreich 1985: 110 Fachleute analysieren unsere Zukunft. Wien: Orac, 1976. xx, 372 p. DB17.S58
    Papers of a project of the Österreichische Gesellschaft für Zukunftspolitik.
Includes bibliographical references.

122

Steininger, Rudolf. Polarisierung und Integration: eine vergleichende Untersuchung der strukturellen Versäulung der Gesellschaft in den Niederlanden und in Österreich. Meisenheim am Glan: A. Hain, 1975. 373 p. (Politik und Wähler; Bd. 14). DJ216.S73
Bibliography: p. 345–373.

123

Suppan, Arnold. Die österreichischen Volksgrupen: Tendenzen ihrer gesellschaftlichen Entwicklung im 20. Jahrhundert. München: R. Oldenbourg, 1983. 262. [7] p.: maps. DB33.S87 1983
Includes indexes.
Bibliography: p. 229–250.

124

Von der Glückseligkeit des Staates: Staat, Wirtschaft und Gesellschaft in Österreich im Zeitalter des aufgeklärten Absolutismus/ herausgegeben von Herbert Matis. Berlin: Duncker & Humbolt, 1981. 558 p.   HC265.V66 1981
   Based on a colloquium held in Vienna, Oct. 1980.
   Bibliography: p. 523-558.

FEDERAL REPUBLIC OF GERMANY

Bibliographies and Reference Works

125

Archer, R. W. A bibliography on land pooling/ readjustment/redistribution for planned urban development in Asia and West Germany. Monticello, Ill.: Vance Bibliographies, 1981. 11 p. (Public administration series — Bibliography)   Z5942.A73

126

Bach, Lüder. Urban and regional planning in West Germany: a bibliography of source material in the English language. Chicago, Ill.: CPL Bibliographies, 1980. 25 p.   Z5942.B26
   Introd. in English and German.

127

Bergmann, Rolf. Bibliographie zur Namenforschung, Mundartforschung und historischen Sprachwissenschaft Bayerisch-Schwabens. München, Vogel, 1978. 103 p. (Schwäbische Geschichtsquellen und Forschungen; 11. Bd.) (Schriften der Philosophischen Fachbereiche der Universität Augsburg; Nr. 13).   DD801.B52A3 Bd. 11
   Includes index.

128

Die Beziehungen zwischen Lateinamerika und der Bundesrepublik Deutschland = Las Relaciones América Latina—República Federal de Alemania. 2. aktualisierte und erg. Aufl. Hamburg: Institut für Iberoamerika-Kunde, Dokumentations-Leitstelle Lateinamerika, 1980. vii, 47 p. (Dokumentationsdienst Lateinamerika. Kurzbibliographie = Documentación Latinoamericana. Introducción bibliográfica)
                       Z1609.R4B49 1980
   English, German, Portuguese, Russian, and Spanish.

129

Bibliographie zur deutschen Soziologie, 1945–1977 = Bibliography of German sociology 1945–1977/Center for Internat. Comparative Studies (CICS) Univ. of Illinois Urbana u. Informationszentrum Sozialwiss. Bonn: hrsg. u. eingel. von Karl-Heinrich Bette, Matthias Herfurth, Günther Lüschen, unter Mitarb. von Gerhard Schönfeld . . . et al. Göttingen: Schwartz, 1980. xvi, 800 p. Z7164.S68B53
Includes indexes.

130

Bibliographie zur Deutschlandpolitik 1941–1974/bearb. von Marie-Luise Goldbach . . . et al./hrsg. vom Bundesministerium für Innerdeutsche Beziehungen. Frankfurt am Main, A. Metzner, 1975. 248 p. (Dokumente zur Deutschlandpolitik: Beihefte; Bd. 1)
Z2240.3.B5
Includes index.

131

Biographisches Handbuch der deutschsprachigen Emigration nach 1933/ Leitung und Bearbeitung, Werner Röder . . . et al. München; New York; K. G. Saur; Detroit, Mich.: Distributed by Gale Research Company, 1980. v. 1. DD68.B52 1980
Half title, v. 1: International biographical dictionary of central European emigrés, 1933–1945.
Bibliography: v. 1, p. 871–875.

132

Bock, Ulla, 1950– Thema Frau: Bibliographie der deutschsprachigen Literatur zur Frauenfrage 1949–1979. Bielefeld: AJZ-Druck und Verlag, 1980. xxxx, 293 p. Z7961.B68

133

Dapper, Karl-Peter. Bibliographie zur sozialen Marktwirtschaft: die Wirtschafts- und Gesellschaftsordnung der Bundesrepublik Deutschland 1945–1981. Baden-Baden: Nomos Verlagsgesellschaft, 1983. xv, 269 p. Z7165.G3D36 1983
Includes index.

134

Dearden, Fay. The German researcher: how to get the most out of an L-D-S branch genealogy library. Minneapolis, Minn. (2912 Orchard Ave. N., Minneapolis 55422): Family Tree Press, 1983. i. 38 p.: ill.
CS614.D4 1983
Bibliography and filmography: p. 36.

135

Deutscher Bibliothekartag (71st: 1981: Regensburg, Germany) Bestände in wissenschaftlichen Bibliotheken: Erschliessung und Erhaltung: Deutscher Bibliothekartag in Regensburg vom 9. bis 13. Juni 1981/ herausgegeben von Jürgen Hering und Eberhard Zwink. Frankfurt am Main: Klostermann, 1982. 269 p.: ill. (Zeitschrift für Bibliothekswesen und Bibliographie. Sonderheft; 34)

Z672.5.D48 1981

Includes bibliographies.

136

Germany (West). Bundesarchiv. Das Bundesarchiv und seine Bestände/ begr. von Friedrich Facius, Hans Booms, Heinz Boberach. 3., erg. u. neubearb. Aufl. Boppard am Rhein, Boldt, 1977. lxxi, 940 p.: ill. (Schriften des Bundesarchivs; Bd. 10).   CD1226.G47 1977

137

Geschichte der Bundesrepublik Deutschland in Quellen und Dokumenten/herausgegeben von Georg Fülberth. Köln: Pahl-Rugenstein, 1982. 449 p. "Literatur- und Quellenverzeichnis"— p. 441-444.   DD259.G465 1982

Includes index.

138

Hahn, Gerhard, 1932- Bibliographie zur Geschichte der CDU und CSU, 1945-1980. Stuttgart: Klett-Cotta, 1982. lxviii, 961 p. (Forschungen und Quellen zur Zeitgeschichte; Bd. 4)   Z7164.P8H34 1982

Includes indexes.

Bibliography: p. xxxiii-lxviii.

139

Handbuch der deutschen Lateinamerika-Forschung Institutionen, Wissenschaftler und Experten in der Bundesrepublik Deutschland und Berlin (West): neuere Veröffentlichungen/ zusammengestellt von Renate Ferno und Wolfgang Grenz. Hamburg: Bonn: Deutscher Akademischer Austauschdienst, 1980. xvii, 483 p.

F1409.95.G3H36

Text also in Portuguese and Spanish.

Includes indexes.

140

Historisches Gemeindeverzeichnis für die Bundesrepublik Deutschland: Namens-, Grenz- und Schlüsselnummernänderungen bei Gemeinden, Kreisen und Regierungsbezirken vom 27.5.1970 bis 31.12.1982/

Herausgeber, Statistisches Bundesamt Wiesbaden. Stuttgart: Kohlhammer, 1983. 815 p.: ill.   DD258.7.H57 1983

141

Hoffmann, Traute. Ausländer in der Bundesrepublik Deutschland: Auswahlbibliographie mit Annotationen. Bonn: Hauptabteilung Wissenschaftliche Dienste der Verwaltung des Deutschen Bundestages, 1982. vi, 158 p. (Bibliographien/ Deutscher Bundestag, Verwaltung, Hauptabteilung Wissenschaftliche Dienste; Nr. 53)

Z7161.G4 Nr. 53

Text in English, French, and German.
Includes index.

142

Institut für Auslandsbeziehungen. Bibliothek. Die auswärtige Kulturpolitik der Bundesrepublik Deutschland: Grundlagen, Ziele, Aufgaben: eine Titelsammlung/ zusammengestellt von Udo Rossbach unter Mitarbeit der Bibliothek des Instituts für Auslandsbeziehungen. Stuttgart: Das Institut, 1980. 207 p. (Schriftenreihe des Instituts für Auslandsbeziehungen: Reihe Dokumentation; Bd. 11)

Z2247.R4I57 1980

Includes index.

143

Lexikon der Ausbildungspraxis/ hrsg. von Helmut Paulik in Zusammenarbeit mit Reinhard Geppert, Horst Gröner und Franz Wagner. 2., überarb. u. erw. Aufl. München: Verlag Moderne Industrie, 1980. 253 p.   LB15.L476 1980
Bibliography: p. 246–252.

144

Literaturbetrieb in der Bundesrepublik Deutschland: ein kritisches Handbuch/ hrsg. von Heinz Ludwig Arnold. 2., völlig veränderte Aufl. München: Edition Text + Kritik, 1981. 420 p.

Z313.L75 1981

Rev. ed. of: Literaturbetrieb in Deutschland. 1971.
Includes bibliographical references.

145

Müller-Lankow, Brigitte. Alternativbewegungen, Protest: von den Studentenunruhen bis zur neuen Jugendbewegung: eine Dokumentation von Forschungsarbeiten und Literatur. Bonn: Informationszentrum Sozialwissenschaften, 1982. 220 leaves.   Z7164.Y8M84 1982
Includes indexes.

146

Philpott, Bryan. The encyclopedia of German military aircraft. New York: Crescent Books, 1981.   UF1245.G4P47
Not presently in LC collections.

147

Reich-Juhr, Hannelore, 1934– Das Gesundheitswesen in der Bundesrepublik Deutschland und in anderen Ländern 1970–1975: Ausw.-Bibliogr. Bonn. Dt. Bundestag, Wiss. Dienste, 1976. vi, 111 p. (Bibliographien-Deutscher Bundestag, Wissenschaftliche Dienste; Nr. 47)   Z7161.G4 Nr. 47
    Includes index.
    Contains a selection of 1820 titles from the holdings of the Bibliothek of the Deutsche Bundestag.

148

Römer, Paul. Schrifttum über den Bundesrat der Bundesrepublik Deutschland und seine unmittelbaren Vorläufer: eine Auswahlbibliographie. Bonn: Direktor das Bundesrates, 1982. viii, 151 p.
    Z7165.G3R65 1982
    Includes index.

149

Rostankowski, Peter. Aktuelle Bibliographie deutsch-, englisch- und französischsprachiger Arbeiten zur Geographie Osteuropas. Berlin: Osteuropa-Institut; Wiesbaden: In Kommission bei Otto Harrassowitz, 1978–1982. 2 v.
    (Bibliographische Mitteilungen des Osteuropa-Instituts an der Freien Unversität Berlin; Heft 17, 23)   Z2483.R66
    Includes indexes.

150

Thode, Ernest. Address book for Germanic genealogy. 2nd ed. Marietta, OH. (R.R.7, Box 306, Marietta 45750): E. Thode, 1980. 1979. iii leaves, 64 p.: map.   CS611.T48 1980

151

Thränhardt, Dietrich. Bibliographie Bundesrepublik Deutschland. Göttingen: Vandenhoeck & Ruprecht, 1980. 178 p. (Arbeitsbücher zur modernen Geschichte; Bd. 9)   Z2221.T5 1980

Description and Travel

315

Alte Burgen, schöne Schlösser: eine romantische Deutschlandreise. Stuttgart; Zürich; Wien: Verlag Das Beste, 1980. 279 p.: chiefly ill. (some col.) DD20.A59

153

Bauernhäuser aus Oberbayern und angrenzenden Gebieten Tirols/herausgegeben von Otto Aufleger. Hannover: Vincentz, 1981. xvi, 8 p., 75 leaves of plates: chiefly ill. (2 col.).
NA8210.B38 1981
Reprint. Originally published: München: L. Werner, 1904.
Includes bibliographic references.

154

Baumgartner, Georg. Königliche Träume: Ludwig II. und seine Bauten. München: Hugendubel, 1981. 260 p.: ill. (some col.)
NA7740.B37 1981
Bibliography: p. 259–260.

155

Bayerische Verwaltung der Staatlichen Schlösser, Gärten und Seen. Schleissheim: neues Schloss und Garten: amtlicher Führer. 6., (veränderte) Aufl. München: Bayerische Verwaltung der Staatlichen Schlösser, Gärten und Seen, 1980. 68 p., 26 p. of plates: ill. (some col.), 1 map. NA7741.S32B39 1980
Summary in English.
Includes index.

156

Burgen und Schlösser in Deutschland. Ostfildern (Kemnat): Mairs Geographischer Verlag, 1982. 288 p.: ill. (chiefly col.)
NA7740.B87 1982
Two maps on folded leaf laid in.

157

Deutschlands schönste Ferienstrassen/hrsg. von Klaus Viedebantt. Hamburg: Hoffmann und Campe, 1981. 303 p.: maps. DD16.D43
Contains articles originally published in the weekly Zeit.
Includes index.

158

Elbin, Günther. Wittelsbacher Schlösser am Rhein und in Westfalen. Duisburg: Mercator-Verlag, 1981. 80 p.: ill. NA7740.E4 1981

159

Evans, Craig, 1949– On foot through Europe, a trail guide to Europe's

long-distance footpaths. New York: Quill, 1982. xiii, 216 p.: ill.
GV199.44.E8E93 1982
Bibliography: p. 203–216

160

Fischer, Bernd, 1935– Wasserburgen im Münsterland. Köln: DuMont.
1980. 205 p.: numerous ill. (some col.)   NA7740.F57
"Erstveröffentlichung."
Includes index.
Bibliography: p. 39

161

Grunsky-Peper, Konrad. Sakrale Kunst in Nordfriesland: Silber, Messing, Zinn. Husum: Husum Druck- und Verlagsgesellschaft, 1982.
168 p.: chiefly ill.   NK7215.G7 1982
Published on the occasion of an exhibition with the same title held
in Husum in the summer of 1982.
Includes index.
Bibliography: p. 166.

162

Herzog, Harald, 1947– Rheinische Schlossbauten im 19. Jahrhundert.
Köln: Rheinland-Verlag; Bonn: In Kommission bei R. Habelt. 1981.
181 p.: ill. (Arbeitsheft/ Landeskonservator Rheinland; 37)
NA7740.B47 1981
Originally presented as the author's thesis (doctoral)—Universität
Köln, 1979.
Bibliography: p. 81–85.

163

Hirschfeld, Peter, 1900– Herrenhäuser und Schlösser in Schleswig-Holstein. München; Berlin: Deutscher Kunstverlag, 1980. vi, 249, 146 p.:
ill., map, plans.   NA7350.S3H5 1980
Includes indexes.
Bibliography: p. 249.

164

Jamieson, Ian. The Simon and Schuster pocket guide to German wines.
New York: Simon and Schuster, 1984.   TP559.G3J35 1984
Not presently in LC collections.
Includes index.

27

165

Klöckner, Karl. Der Fachwerkbau in Hessen. München: Callwey, 1980.
226 p.: numerous ill. (some col.)   NA1075.K56
    Includes index.
    Bibliography: 223–224.

166

Kreft, Herbert. Die Weserrenaissance. 5., überarb. und erw. Aufl.
Hameln: CW Niemeyer. 1980. 324 p.: chiefly ill. (some col.) 2 fold.
maps (in pocket).   NA1082.W38K73 1980
    Legends in English and German.
    Includes bibliographical references and index.

167

Leuschner, Peter, 1947– Romanische Kirchen in Bayern. Pfaffenhofen:
W. Ludwig, 1981. 206 p.: ill. (some col.).   NA5573.L47 1981
    Bibliography: p. 205–206.

168

Petzoldt, Leander. Volkstümliche Feste: ein Führer zu Volksfesten,
Märkten und Messen in Deutschland. München: C. H. Beck, 1983.
483 p.: ill.   GT4850.A2F47 1983
    Includes index.
    Bibliography: p. 461–470.

169

Pieroth, Kuno F., 1937– The great German wine book. New York: Ster-
ling Pub. Co., 1983. 208 p.: ill. (some col.)
                        TP559.G3P5313 1983
    Translation of: Das grosse Buch der deutschen Weinkultur.
    Includes index.

170

Rohrberg, Erwin. Schöne Fachwerkhäuser in Baden-Württemberg. Stuttgart: DRW-Verlag, 1981. 143 p.: ill. (some col.)
                        NA1072.B23R63 1981
    Bibliography: p. 142.

171

Rumohr, Henning von. Schlösser und Herrenhäuser im nördlichen und
westlichen Holstein: ein Handbuch mit 115 Aufnahmen und 8 Farbtafeln. Frankfurt am Main: W. Weidlich, 1981. 317 p.: ill. (some col.).
2 maps.   NA7740.R85 1981
    Map on lining paper.
    Includes index.

172

Rumohr, Henning von. Schlösser und Herrenhäuser in Ostholstein: ein
Handbuch mit 155 Aufnahmen und 8 Farbtafeln. 2., überarbeitete und
erw. Aufl. Frankfurt am Main: Weidlich, 1982, 1973. 442 p.: 163 ill.
(8 col.)   DD801.H73R85 1982
Includes index.

173

Scheidulin, Hans. Alte Kirchen in und um Bremen: Kunstschätze im
Weserraum. Bremen: Schünemann, 1982. 144 p.: col. ill.
                                                 NA5586.B717S34 1982
Bibliography: p. 144.

174

Schilling, Richard. Das alte malerische Schwarzwald-Haus: eine
Schilderung der verschiedenen Bauarten des Äusseren und Inneren
des Schwarzwaldhauses unter besonderer Berücksichtigung der alten
handwerksmässigen Volkskunst sowie die Sitten und Gebräuche seiner
Bewohner. Freiburg im Breisgau: Verlag K. Schillinger, 1981. xii,
160 p., [1] leaf of plates: ill.   NA8210.G3S33 1981
Reprint. Originally published: Freiburg: Commissions-Verlag der
Freiburger Druck- und Verlagsgesellschaft, 1915.

175

Schöck, Inge. Häuser und Landschaften in Baden-Württemberg: Tradi-
tion und Wandel ländlicher Baukultur. Stuttgart: W. Kohlhammer,
1982. 160 p.: ill. (some col.), maps.   NA7350.B24S36 1982
Maps on lining paper.
Includes index.
Bibliography: p. 147–155.

176

Schönes Deutschland, neu erlebt: 100 Autotouren u. 380 Wanderungen.
Stuttgart; Zürich; Wien: Verlag Das Beste, 1980. 480 p.: numerous
ill. (chiefly col.).   DD16.S36
"Begleitbuch" 103 p.: all col. maps inserted in pocket.
Includes index.

177

Schoonmaker, Frank, 1905– The wines of Germany: Frank Schoonmaker's classic. Completely rev. ed. New York: Hastings House, 1980.
223 p.: ill.   TP559.G3S3 1980
Includes index.
Bibliography: p. 213–214.

178

Stoermer, Hans W. Zimmererkunst am Bauernhaus: bayrischalpines
Bundwerk. Regensburg: Pustet, 1980. 111 p.: ill., maps.

NK9650.A3B387

Includes index.
Bibliography: p. 104–105.

179

Strieffler, Heinrich, 1872–1949. Fröhlich' Pfalz, Gott erhalt's! 2. erw.
Aufl. Landau in der Pfalz: Verlag Pfälzer Kunst, 1981. 124 p.: chiefly
ill. (some col.). TP559.G3S87 1981
"Die Beiträge zu diesen Buch schrieben: Theo Becker . . . et al."
Includes bibliographical references.

180

Tour of W. Germany (including East Berlin): a comprehensive travel
guide and a reference book to travel publications. Denver, Colo. (217
W. First Ave., Denver 80223): Oro Press, 1981. v., 188 p., [1] folded
leaf of plates: ill. (some col.), maps (some col.). DD16.T57

181

Volk, Helmut. Skilanglauf als Freizeitsport: ein Beitrag zur Erforschung
der Erholungsnutzung der Wälder. Freiburg: Forstliche Versuchs- und
Forschungsanstalt Baden-Württemberg, 1981. 81 p.: ill., maps.

GV854.8.G4V64 1981

(Mitteilungen der Forstlichen Versuchs- und Forschungsanstalt
Baden-Württemberg; Heft 96)
Bibliography: p. 79–81.

182

Wehrmann, Volker. Burgen, Schlösser, Herrensitze, Kirchen, Bauern-
höfe, Bürgerhäuser in Lippe. 2. Aufl. Detmold: Lippischer Heimat-
bund, 1981. 200 p.: ill. (some col.). NA1076.L56W43 1981
Folded col. map in pocket.

183

Werner-Künzig, Waltraut. Schwarzwälder Trachten = Traditional
costumes in the Black Forest. Karlsruhe: Badenia, 1981. 96 p.: chiefly
ill. (some col.). GT920.W47 1981
Parallel text in English, French, and German.
Includes index.
Bibliography: p. 96.

184

Woschek, Heinz-Gert. Der deutsche Weinführer: das Deutschland-

Weinbuch. 4., überarb. Aufl. München: Mvg, 1980, 1970. 333 p.:
col. ill., maps.   TP559.G3W74 1980
Includes index.

Economy

185

Bace, Lynn A. Coping with inflation: experiences of financial executives
in the United Kingdom, Brazil, and West Germany: a research study
and report, prepared for Financial Executives Research Foundation
by Lynn A. Bace, Edward H. Schwallie, Gary W. Silverman. New
York, N. Y.: The Foundation, 1981. xiii, 103 p.: ill.
                                                    HD49.5.B3 1981
Bibliography: p. 95-103.

186

Beckermann, Theo. Das Handwerk in der Bundesrepublik Deutschland.
Berlin: Duncker & Humblot, 1980. 252 p.: ill.
                                                    HD2346.G3B386 1980
Includes bibliographical references.

187

Boigk, Heinz. Erdöl und Erdölgas in der Bundesrepublik Deutschland:
Erdölprovinzen, Felder, Förderung, Vorräte, Lagerstättentechnik.
Stuttgart: Enke, 1981. x, 330 p.: ill., maps (2 folded)
                                                    TN874.G4B64
Includes bibliographies and indexes.

188

Boss, Alfred. On the economic development in the Federal Republic of
Germany in the 1980's: outline for two scenarios. Kiel: Institut für
Weltwirtschaft, 1981. 84 p.: ill.   HC286.7.B6813 1981
(Kieler Arbeitspapiere; Arbeitspapier Nr. 134 = Kiel working
papers) Updated translation of Zur wirtschaftlichen Entwicklung in
der Bundesrepublik Deutschland in den achtziger Jahren.
Includes bibliographical references.

189

The British and German banking system: a comparative study/prepared
by Economists Advisory Group Ltd. for the Anglo-German Foundation. London: The Foundation, 1981, xx, 419 p.
                                                    HG2988.B75 1981
Bibliography: p. 409-418.

190

Deutsch-afrikanische Industriekooperationen in der Rohstoffwirtschaft: Industriegespräch der DEG mit dem Club von Dakar. Köln: DEG, Deutsche Gesellschaft für Wirtschaftliche Zusammenarbeit (Entwicklungsgesellschaft), 1980. 84 p. (DEG Materialien; 7)

HD9506.A382D48

Papers presented at a meeting organized by the Deutsche Gesellschaft für Wirtschaftliche Zusammenarbeit (Entwicklungsgesellschaft) mbH, the Club de Dakar, and the Deutsche Stiftung für Internationale Entwicklung.

Includes bibliographical references.

191

Ehmann-Schneider, Sybill. Marketing the U. S. travel product: selling to Germany. Washington, D. C. (1899 L Street, N. W., Washington, D. C. 20036): Travel Industry Association of America, 1982, v, 49 p.: ill. G155.U6E37 1982

192

Feld, Werner J. West Germany and the European Community: changing interests and competing policy objectives. New York: Praeger. 1981. x, 151 p. HC241.25.G3F44

Includes bibliographical references.

193

Franz, Wolfgang, 1905– Youth unemployment in the Federal Republic of Germany: theory, empirical results, and policy implications: an economic analysis. Tübingen: J.C.B. Mohr, 1982. vii, 258 p.: ill. (Schriften zur Umwelt- und Ressourcenökonomie, Bd. 6)

HD6276.G4F72 1982

Bibliography: p. 238–258.

194

Fuchs, Gerhard, 1939– Die Bundesrepublik Deutschland: Neubearbeitung. Stuttgart: E. Klett, 1983. 296 p.: ill. (1 col.), maps. (Länderprofile, geographische Strukturen, Daten, Entwicklungen)

HD656.F8 1983

Two col. maps on folded leaf in pocket.

Includes index.

Bibliography: p. 282–292.

195

German trade fairs: a handbook for American exporters/ Patrick Killough, editor. Washington, D. C.: U. S. Dept. of Commerce, International

Trade Administration: For sale by the Supt. of Docs., U. S. G.P.O.,
1981. v, 99 p.   T395.G4G47
"American Embassy, Bonn."
"May 1981"—Cover.
Bibliography: p. 95-96.

196
The Germans—public opinion polls, 1967-1980/ edited by Elisabeth
Noelle-Neumann; Institut für Demoskopie Allensbach. Westport,
Conn.: Greenwood Press, 1981. xviii, 516 p.: ill.
                                                           HN460.P8G47
Includes index.

197
Görgens, Egon, 1941- Beschäftigungspolitik. München: Vahlen, 1981.
viii, 166 p.   HD5779.G62 1981
Includes bibliographical references and index.

198
Hegelheimer, Barbara. Equal opportunities and vocational training: training and labour market policy measures for the vocational promotion
of women in the Federal Republic of Germany. Berlin: European Centre for the Development of Vocational Training, 1981, 1982. v, 307 p.
                                                      HD6059.6.G4H43 1982
"Contribution of the Federal Republic of Germany to a survey con-
ducted in the member states of the European Communities on behalf
of the European Centre for the Development of Vocational Training
(CEDEFOP), Berlin, 1979."
Includes bibliographical references.

199
Horn, Ernst-Jürgen. Management of industrial change in the Federal
Republic of Germany. Brighton: Sussex European Research Centre,
University of Sussex, 1982. vi, 134 p. (Sussex European papers; no.
13) (Industrial adjustment and policy; 4)
                                                      HD3616.G35H62 1982
Includes bibliographical references.

200
Job sharing: flexible Arbeitszeit durch Arbeitsplatzteilung/ H.-Helmut
Heymann, Lothar J. Seiwert (Hrsg.) Grafenau/Württ. Expert-Verlag,
1982. 492 p.: ill.   HD5110.6.G3J6 1982
Bibliography: p. 471-483.

201

Kontrolle von Marktmacht nach deutschem, europäischem und amerikanischem Kartellrecht: Referate eines FIW-Kolloquiums. Köln: C. Heymanns Verlag, 1981. viii, 176 p.   HB41.F22 Heft 98
English and German.
Includes bibliographical references.

202

Kräger, Horst. Infrastruktur, technischer Fortschritt und Wirtschaftswachstum: eine ökonomische und kontrolltheoretische Untersuchung für den Industriebereich der Bundesrepublik Deutschland. Thun; Frankfurt am Main: Deutsch, 1980. iii, 184 p.: ill. (Reihe Wirtschaftswissenschaften; Bd. 192)   HC286.7.K72 1980
Originally presented as the author's thesis (doctoral)—Universität Mannheim, 1979.
Bibliography: p. 172–184.

203

Kühl, Jürgen. Employment policy in Germany: challenges and concepts for the 1980's. 2nd ed. Nürnberg: Federal Employment Institute, 1980. 192 p.: ill.   HD5779.K7913 1980
Translation of: Überlegungen zu einer vorausschauenden Arbeitsmarktpolitik.
Includes index.
Bibliography: p. 184–189.

204

Lawrence, Peter A. Managers and management in West Germany. New York: St. Martin's Press, 1980. 202 p.   HD70.G2L38 1980
Includes index.
Bibliography: p. 191–198.

205

Lehment, Harmen. Exchange-market interventions and monetary policy: the German experience. Kiel: Kiel Institute of World Economics, 1980. 35 leaves: ill. (Kiel working papers; no. 111)   HG3949.L4
Bibliography: p. 34–35.

206

Lübbers, Ralf. Inflation, Beschäftigung und rationale Erwartungen. Berlin: Duncker & Humblot, 1981. 221 p.   HD5710.L8 1981
Summary in English, French, and German.
Includes index.
Bibliography: p. 201–218.

207

Michaels, Heinz. Made in Japan, made in Germany: wie die deutsche Automobilindustrie der japanischen Herausforderung begegnet. Düsseldorf: Econ Verlag, 1981. 80 p.   HC290.5.I52M52 1981

208

Nardozzi, Giangiacomo. Structural trends of financial systems and capital accumulation: France, Germany, Italy. Brussels, Belgium: Directorate-General for Economic and Financial Affairs, Commission of the European Communities, 1983. 104 p.: ill. (Economic papers; no. 14)
                                                    HG186.F8N37 1983
 "May 1983."
 "Internal paper."
 Includes bibliographical references.

209

Neipp, Joachim W. Zur Bedeutung der Input-Output Analyse für eine Statistik des Aussenhandels: dargestellt am Beispiel d. Bundesrepublik Deutschland u.d. Niederlande. Frankfurt/M.: R. G. Fischer, 1980. 238, [48] p.: graphs. (Schriften zur q[u]antitativen Wirtschaftsforschung; Bd. 2)   HF3566.5.N43 1980
 Originally presented as the author's thesis, Heidelberg under title: Die Darstellung und kritische Würdigung des statistischen Instrumentariums zur Analyse des Aussenhandels unter besonderer Berücksichtigung der Input-Output-Analyse.
 Bibliography: p. 42–48 (2d group).

210

Overy, R. J. The Nazi economic recovery, 1932–1938/ prepared for the Economic History Society by R. J. Overy. London: Macmillan Press, 1982. 76 p. (Studies in economic and social history)
                                                    HC286.3.O94 1982
 Includes index.
 Bibliography: p. 67–74.

211

Owen Smith, E. The West German economy. New York: St. Martin's Press, 1983. 331 p.: ill.   HC286.5.O93 1983
 Includes index.
 Bibliography: p. 303–317.

212

Paul-Calm, Hanna. Ostpolitik und Wirtschaftsinteressen in der Ära Adenauer, 1955–1963. FrankfurtMain; New York: Campus Verlag, 1981. 295 p.   HF1546.15.E852P38 1981
 Bibliography: p. 256–295.

213

Peacock, Alan T., 1922- Structural economic policies in West Germany and the United Kingdom. London: Anglo-German Foundation for the Study of Industrial Society, 1980. iv, 128 p.   HC286.P42 1980
"The research for this publication was financed by the Anglo-German Foundation for the Study of Industrial Society."
Includes bibliographies.

214

Prais, S. J. Productivity and industrial structure: a statistical study of manufacturing industry in Britain, Germany, and the United States. New York: Cambridge University Press, 1981. xix, 401 p. (Economic and social studies/ National Institute of Economic and Social Research; 33)   HC79.I52P7 1981
Includes index.
Bibliography: p. 379-390.

215

Schwartz, Gail Garfield. Urban economic development in Great Britain and West Germany: lessons for the United States. Columbus, Ohio: Academy for Contemporary Problems, 1980. vi, 9 p.
HT178.G7S38
"A report of the Trinational Cities Exchange."

216

Smith, Anthony Douglas, 1933- International industrial productivity: a comparison of Britain, America, and Germany. Cambridge [Cambridgeshire]; New York: Cambridge University Press, 1982. xiv, 170 p.: ill. (Occasional papers/ the National Institute of Economic and Social Research; 34)   HC260.I52S6 1982
Includes bibliographical references and index.

217

Stent, Angela. From embargo to Ostpolitik: the political economy of West German-Soviet relations, 1955-1980. Cambridge; New York: Cambridge University Press, 1981. xvi, 328 p. (Soviet and East European studies)   HF1546.15.S63S73
Includes index.
Bibliography: p. 304-315.

218

Striner, Herbert E. Regaining the lead: policies for economic growth. New York, N. Y.: Praeger, 1984. xvii, 205 p.
HC106.8.S77 1984
Includes bibliographical references and index.

219

Trommer, Luitgard. Ausländer in der Bundesrepublik Deutschland: Dokumentation und Analyse amtlicher Statistiken. München: DJI Verlag Deutsches Jugendinstitut, 1981. 235 p.: ill.

HA1244.T76 1981

Bibliography: p. 164.

220

Wannenmacher, Walter. Die zweite Weltwirtschaftskrise: Fakten und Folgerungen. Stuttgart: Deutsche Verlags-Anstalt, 1983. 231 p.: ill.

HC59.W28 1983

221

Weiss, Frank Dietmar. The structure of international competitiveness in the Federal Republic of Germany: an appraisal. Washington, D. C.: World Bank, 1983. 64 p.   HF1545.W42 1983

Bibliography: p. 53–64.

222

Weiss, Frank Dietmar. West Germany's trade with the East: hypotheses and perspectives. Tübingen: J.C.B. Mohr, 1983. xi, 109 p.: ill.. (Kieler Studien, 179)   HF3568.E35W44 1983

Bibliography: p.. 94–109.

223

West Germany, a European and global power/ edited by Wilfrid L. Kohl, Giorgio Basevi. Lexington, Mass.: Lexington Books, 1980. xv, 224 p.: graphs.   HF1545.W45

Based on papers presented at a conference held at the Bologna Center of Johns Hopkins University, Oct. 5–7, 1978.

Includes bibliographical references.

224

Wolter, Frank. The impact of manufactured imports from developing countries in the Federal Republic of Germany. Kiel: Institut für Weltwirtschaft an der Universität Kiel, 1980. 34 leaves. (Kiel working papers; no. 99)   HD5779.W72

Bibliography: leaves 33–34.

Intellectual and Cultural Life

225

Die Alternativpresse: Kontroversen, Polemiken, Dokumente/ hrsg. von Günther Emig, Peter Engel & Christoph Schubert. Ellwangen: G. Emig

[Selbstverl.], 1980. x, 271 p.: ill.   PN5214.U53A44
500 copies printed.
Bibliography: p. 254–262.

226
Architektur in Deutschland '81: deutscher Architekturpreis 1981/
herausgegeben von Ruhrgas AG Essen und Jürgen Joedicke. Stuttgart:
K. Krämer, 1982. 99 p.: ill. (some col.)   NA1068.A676 1982

227
Ausländerkinder im Konflikt: zur interkulturellen Arbeit in Schule und
Gemeinwesen/ Helmut Essinger, Achim Hellmich, Gerd Hoff (Hrsg.)
Königstein/Ts.: Athenäum, 1981. 215 p.: ill.
                                        LC5158.G3A94 1981
Bibliography: p. 148–149.

228
Ausländische Kinder und Jugendliche im deutschen Bildungs- und
Ausbildungssystem: Probleme, Programme, Erfahrungen. Köln:
Deutscher Städtetag, 1980. 181 p.: ill. (Zweite Ausländergeneration;
T. 2) (Reihe C, DST-Beiträge zur Bildungspolitik; Heft 12)
                                        LC5158.G3Z93 1980 T.2

229
Bellut, Thomas. Die DDR-Berichterstattung in den Nachrichtenmedien
der Bundesrepublik Deutschland. Münster: Lit Verlag, 1983. v, v,
316 p.: ill.   PN5214.F67B45 1983
Bibliography: p. 304–316.

230
Bildung in der Bundesrepublik Deutschland: Daten u. Analysen/ Max-
Planck-Inst. für Bildungsforschung. Stuttgart: Klett-Cotta, 1980. v.
1: ill.   LA721.82.B5
Includes bibliographies.
Contents—Bd. 1. Entwicklungen seit 1950.

231
Bildungswesen in der Bundesrepublik Deutschland. English. Between elite
and mass education: education in the Federal Republic of Germany/
Max Planck Institute for Human Development and Education, Berlin,
Federal Republic of Germany. Albany: State University of New York
Press, 1983, c1979.   LC93.G4B55313 1983
Not presently in LC collections.
Translation of: Das Bildungswesen in der Bundesrepublik
Deutschland.

232

Clyne, Michael G., 1939- Language and society in the German-speaking countries. Cambridge [Cambridgeshire]; New York: Cambridge University Press, 1984.   PF3973.C55 1984
Not presently in LC collections.
Includes indexes.

233

Cologne, Kunstgewerbemuseum. Europäisches Porzellan und ostasiatisches Exportporzellan, Geschirr und Ziergerät/ von Barbara Beaucamp-Markowsky; Kunstgewerbemuseum der Stadt Köln. Köln: Das Museum, 1980. 515 p.: ill. (Kataloge des Kunstgewerbemuseums Köln; Bd. 6)   NK480.C73A3 Bd. 6
Includes index.
Bibliography: p. 489-506.

234

The Compleat university: break from tradition in Germany, Sweden, and the U.S.A./ Harry Hermanns, Ulrich Teichler, Henry Wasser, editors. Cambridge, Mass.: Schenkman, 1983. xii, 322 p.
                    LB2341.8.G3C65 1983
Papers presented at a conference held in Dec. 1980 in New York and a second one held in Sept. 1981 in Kassel.
"A publication of the Center for European Studies, Graduate School, City University of New York."
Includes bibliographical references.

235

Contemporary German prints, constructivists, realists: 33 artists of the Federal Republic of Germany/ organized by the Institute for Foreign Cultural Relations, Stuttgart; selected by Thomas Grochowiak. Stuttgart: Institute for Foreign Cultural Relations, 1980, 46 p.: ill.
                    NE651.6.C64C6 1980

236

Corrigan, Timothy. New German film: the displaced image. Austin: University of Texas Press, 1983. xiv, 213 p.: ill.
                    PN1993.5.G3C67 1983
Includes index.
Bibliography: p. 203-210.
Filmography: p. 197-201.

237

Daum, Thomas. Die 2. Kultur: Alternativliteratur in der Bundesrepublik.
NewLit Verlag, 1981. 184 p.: ill. (Gutenberg-Syndrom; 2)

Z316.D38 1981

Bibliography: p. 175–183.

238

Deutsche Keramik 82: Westerwaldpreis: Höhr-Grenzhausen,
Keramikmuseum Westerwald, 22. Oktober 1982 bis 30. Januar 1983.
2. Aufl. Montabaur: Die Kreisverwaltung, 1983. 319 p.: chiefly ill.
(some col.). NK4099.D398 1983
Includes index.

239

Deutsche Literatur in der Bundesrepublik seit 1965/ hrsg. von Paul
Michael Lützeler u. Egon Schwarz. Königstein/Ts.: Athenäum, 1980.
318 p. PT403.D395
Includes bibliographical references and index.

240

Der Deutsche Museumsführer in Farbe: Museen und Sammlungen in
der Bundesrepublik Deutschland und West-Berlin/ herausgegeben von
Klemens Mörmann. 2., völlig überarbeitete und erw. Neuausg.
Frankfurt am Main: Krüger, 1983. 1065 p.: col. ill., maps.

AM49.D48 1983

Includes indexes.
Bibliography: p. 1032–1035.

241

Eyssen, Jürgen. Buchkunst in Deutschland: vom Jugendstil zum Maler-
buch: Buchgestalter, Handpressen, Verleger, Illustratoren. Hannover:
Schlütersche, 1980. 245 p.: ill. (some col.) Z116.A3E96
Includes bibliographies and index.

242

Fischer, Robert, 1954– Der neue deutsche Film, 1960–1980.
Originalausg. München: Goldmann, 1981. 289, [1] p.: ill.

PN1997.8.F58 1981

Bibliography: p. 289–290.

243

Fohrbeck, Karla, 1942– Musik, Statistik, Kulturpolitik: Daten und
Argumente zum Musikleben in der Bundesrepublik Deutschland.

Köln: DuMont, 1982. 267 p.: ill. (Kultur und Staat. Studien zur
Kulturpolitik)   ML275.F6 1982
Includes index.

244

German masters of the nineteenth century: paintings and drawings from
the Federal Republic of Germany. New York: Metropolitan Museum
of Art: Distributed by H. N. Abrams, 1981. 280 p.: ill. (some col.).
"Published in connection with an exhibition at the Metropolitan
Museum of Art, New York, from May 2—July 5, 1981, and at the
Art Gallery of Ontario, Canada, from August 1—October 11, 1981."
                                                                    N6867.G47
     Bibliography: p. 275-280

245

Germanistentag (1980: Saarbrücken, Germany) Medien und
Deutschunterricht: Vorträge des Germanistentags, Saarbrücken 1980/
hrsg. von Eduard Schaefer. Tübingen: Niemeyer, 1981. 168 p.: 3 ill.
(Medien in Forschung + Unterricht, Serie B; Bd. 2)
                                                                    PF3068.G43G44 1980
     Partial proceedings.
     Includes bibliographies.

246

Geschichten aus der Geschichte der Bundesrepublik Deutschland
1949-1979/ hrsg. von Klaus Roehler. Darmstadt: Luchterhand, 1980.
411 p.   PT1334.G418
     Contains material previously published in various sources.

247

Hartmann-Laugs, Petra S., 1946- Unterhaltung und Politik im Abend-
programm des DDR-Fernsehens. Köln: Verlag Wissenschaft und
Politik, 1982. 239 p.: ill. (Bibliothek Wissenschaft und Politik; Bd. 29)
                                                                    PN1992.6.H37 1982
     Bibliography: p. 181-188.

248

Hayman, Ronald, 1932- Fassbinder film maker. New York: Simon &
Schuster, 1984.   PN1998.A3F2744 1984
     Not presently in LC collections.

249

Hein, Peter Ulrich. Der Künstler als Sozialtherapeut: Kunst als ideelle
Dienstleistung in der entwickelten Industriegesellschaft. Frankfurt/

Main; New York: Campus Verlag, 1982. 172 p.

NX180.S6H36 1982

Bibliography: p. 165-172.

250

Hickethier, Knut, 1945- Das Fernsehspiel der Bundesrepublik: Themen, Form, Struktur, Theorie und Geschichte; 1951-1977. Stuttgart: Metzler, 1980. ix, 383 p.   PN1992.65.H5 1980

Originally presented as the author's thesis (doctoral—Technische Universität, Berlin, 1979).

Includes bibliography and indexes.

251

Hill, Werner, 1925- Fasnacht: ein Porträt des Narrenspiels in badischpfälzischen Landen. Mannheim: Südwestdeutsche Verlagsanstalt, 1980. 159 p.: numerous ill. (some col.).

GT4250.A3B333 1980

Includes bibliographical references.

252

Hippe, Robert. Trivialliteratur. Hollfeld/Ofr.: Bange, 1981. 120 p.

PT405.H5 1981

Includes bibliographical references.

253

Hochschulreform, und was nun?: Berichte, Glossen, Perspektiven/ Horst Albert Glaser (Hrsg.). Frankfurt/M: Ullstein, 1982. 1981. 478 p.

LA728.7.H62 1982

Includes bibliographical references.

254

Hufnagel, Erwin, 1940- Pädagogische Theorien im 20. Jahrhundert. Frankfurt/ Main: Haag + Herchen, 1982. 188 p.

LA721.8.H83 1982

Includes bibliographies.

255

International Council for Educational Development. Deutsch-Amerikanische Studiengruppe. Hochschulzugang in den USA und der Bundesrepublik Deutschland: Bericht einer deutsch-amerikanischen Studiengruppe des International Council for Educational Development/ hrsg. von James A. Perkins und Barbara B. Burn. Göttingen: Vandenhoeck & Ruprecht, 1980. 270 p. (Schriftenreihe der Stiftung Volkswagenwerk, Bd. 18)   LA728.I488 1980

Bibliography: p. 267-270.

256

Jenseits der deutsch-deutschen Grenze/ Rolf Italiaander [Hrsg.] Stockach/
Bodensee: Weidling, 1981. 142 p.: 90 col. ill.

ND568.5.P67J46

257

Kamphausen, Alfred. Bauernmalerei in Schleswig-Holstein. 2., überarb.
Aufl. Heide in Holstein: Westholsteinische Verlagsanstalt Boyens,
1980. 31, [44] p.: ill. (some col.). NK952.S2K35 1980
Includes bibliographical references.

258

Köttelwesch, Clemens. Das wissenschaftliche Bibliothekswesen in der
Bundesrepublik Deutschland. 2. überarbeitete Aufl. Frankfurt am
Main: Klostermann, 1980. v. 1-2. Z675.R45K63 1980.
Includes bibliographies and indexes.
Contents.— 1. Die Bibliotheken: Aufgaben und Strukturen — 2.
Die Bibliotheken in ihrer Umwelt.

259

Krüger, Hans Joachim. Studentenprobleme: psychosoziale und institutionelle Befunde. Frankfurt/Main; New York: Campus, 1982. 180 p.:
ill. LB3499.G3K78 1982
Bibliography: p. 157-180.

260

Liebold, Christine. Das Rokoko in ursprünglich mittelalterlichen Kirchen des bayerischen Gebietes, ein von maurinischem Denken
geprägter Stil. München: Kommissionsbuchhandlung Wölfle, 1981.
194 p., [6] leaves of plates: ill. (Miscellanea Bavarica Monacensia: Heft
98) (Neue Schriftenreihe des Stadtarchivs München; Bd. Nr. 119)
NA5573.L53 1981
Originally presented as the author's thesis (doctoral)—München,
1979.
Bibliography: p. 181-194.

261

Lundgreen, Peter. Sozialgeschichte der deutschen Schule im Überblick.
Göttingen: Vandenhoeck & Ruprecht, 1980-1981. 2 v.
LC191.8.G3L86 1980
Includes bibliographies and indexes.
Contents.—T. 1. 1770-1918 — T. 2. 1918-1980.

262

Müller, Helmut L. Die literarische Republik: westdeutsche Schriftsteller und die Politik. Weinheim: Beltz, 1982. 343 p.

PT405.M77 1982

A revised edition of the author's thesis (doctoral)—Ludwig-Maximilians-Universität, München, 1980.
Bibliography: p. 323-343.

263

Peisert, Hansgert. Das Hochschulsystem in der Bundesrepublik Deutschland: Funktionsweise und Leistungsfähigkeit. 2., erw. Aufl. Stuttgart: Klett-Cotta, 1980, 1979. 215 p.: ill.   LA728.P43 1980
Bibliography: p. 180-191.

264

Pernkopf, Johannes. Der 17. Juni 1953 in der Literatur der beiden deutschen Staaten. Stuttgart: Akademischer Verlag H.-D. Heinz, 1982. 326 p. (Stuttgarter Arbeiten zur Germanistik; Nr. 123. Salzburger Beiträge; Nr. 6.)   PT405.P38 1982
Originally presented as the author's thesis (doctoral)—Universität Salzburg)
Bibliography: p. 310-326.

265

Preuss, Joachim Werner. Fostering the performing arts in the Federal Republic of Germany. Strasbourg: Council for Cultural Co-operation, 1980. 38 p., [2] p. of plates; maps. (Education & Culture)

PN2044.G4P7

Includes bibliographical references.

266

Recum, Hasso von. Education in the affluent society: its impact on the economics of education, educational policies and reform: three essays. Frankfurt (Main): German Institute for International Educational Research, 1980. 64 p.   LC93.G4R42
Includes bibliographyical references.

267

Reeb, Hans-Joachim. Bildungsauftrag der Schule: eine Analyse der Erziehungsziele in den Verfassungen und Schulgesetzen der Bundesrepublik Deutschland unter Einbeziehung der Richtlinien im Lande Niedersachsen. Frankfurt/Main: R. G. Fischer, 1981. 225 p. (Beiträge zur Bildungspolitik, Bd. 2)   LC93.G4R43 1981
Bibliography: p. 178-195.

268

Reinhold, Ursula. Tendenzen und Autoren: zur Literatur der siebziger Jahre in der BRD. Berlin: Dietz Verlag, 1982. 462 p.

PT401.R44 1982

Includes bibliographical references.

269

Rentschler, Eric. West German film in the course of time: reflections on the twenty years since Oberhausen. Bedford Hills, N. Y.: Redgrave Pub. Co., 1984. PN1993.5.G3R44 1984

Includes index.

Not presently in LC collections.

270

Renz, Peter. Sprach- und Literaturwissenschaft in der Bundesrepublik Deutschland und in der DDR. Erlangen: Institut für Gesellschaft und Wissenschaft, 1981. 115 p. H5.A14 1981, no. 5

Bibliography: p. 113-115.

271

Riesenberger, Dieter, 1938– Geschichtsmuseum und Geschichtsunterricht: Analysen u. Konzepte aus d. Bundesrepublik Deutschland u.d. DDR. Düsseldorf: Pädagogischer Verlag Schwann, 1980. 116 p.: ill., maps. (Geschichte und Sozialwissenschaften) AM7.R48

Includes bibliographical references.

272

Ringholz, Holger. Vom Beruf zur Hochschule: die Berufsoberschule in Bayern. München: Ehrenwirth, 1981. 480 p. ill. LC1047.G3R56

Bibliography: p. 438-440.

273

Rosenthal: Hundert Jahre Porzellan: Ausstellung, Kestner-Museum Hannover/ herausgegeben für das Kestner-Museum Hannover unter wissenschaftlicher Mitarbeit von Helga Hilschenz; bearbeitet von Bernd Fritz. Stuttgart: Union, 1982. 259 p.: ill. (chiefly col.)

NK4210.R555R67 1982

Exhibition held April 29–June 13, 1982.

Includes indexes.

274

Rothman, Stanley, 1927– Roots of radicalism: Jews, Christians, and the New Left. New York: Oxford University Press, 1982. xiv, 466 p.

LB3610.R67 1982

Includes bibliographical references and index.

275

Scharf, Wilfried, 1945- Nachrichten im Fernsehen der Bundesrepublik
Deutschland und der DDR: Objektivität oder Parteilichkeit in der
Berichterstattung. Frankfurt am Main: R. G. Fischer, 1981. iv, 222 p.:
ill., map.   PN5214.T4S38
    Bibliography: p.210-222.

276

Schatzker, Chaim. Die Juden in den deutschen Geschichtsbüchern:
Schulbuchanalyse zur Darstellung der Juden, des Judentums und des
Staates Israel. Bonn: Bundeszentrale für Politische Bildung, 1981.
188 p. (Schriftenreihe der Bundeszentrale für Politische Bildung; Bd.
173)   JN3966.A3 Bd. 173
    Bibliography: p. 182-188.

277

Schmid-Jörg, Ina, 1942- Bildungschancen für Mädchen und Frauen im
internationalen Vergleich: Regelungen zur Absicherung gleicher
Chancen für Mädchen und Frauen im Bildungs- und Berufsbildungs-
bereich: Untersuchung. München; Wien: Oldenbourg, 1981. xvi,
420 p.: ill. (Sozialwissenschaftliche Reihe des Battelle-Instituts e.V.;
Bd. 5)   LC1483.S37 1981

278

Schorb, Alfons Otto. Zur Infrastruktur des Schulwesens. München:
Ehrenwirth, 1980. 75 p. (Studien und Materialien des Staatsinstituts
für Bildungsforschung München; Folge 9)   LB2911.S36
    Includes bibliographical references.

279

Schweitzer, Hartmut. Fachwahl unter Numerus-clausus-Bedingungen.
Köln; Wien: Böhlau, 1981. xvi, 330 p.: ill. (Sozialwissenschaftliches
Forum; 16)   LB2351.4.G3S35 1981
    Bibliography: p. 318-327.

280

Stichworte zur geistigen Situation der Zeit. English. Observations on ''the
spiritual situation of the age'': contemporary German perspectives/
edited by Jürgen Habermas. Cambridge, Mass.: MIT Press, 1984.
(Studies in contemporary German social thought)
                                                     DD259.4.S83313 1984
    Translation of: Stichworte zur geistigen Situation der Zeit.
    Includes bibliographical references and index.
    Not presently in LC collections.

281

Studium und Beruf: zur Studienreform in den Wirtschafts- und Sozialwissenschaften/ Veröffentlichung der Hochschule für Wirtschaft und Politik Hamburg; mit Beiträgen von Norbert Aust . . . et al.]. Opladen: Westdeutscher Verlag, 1981. 269 p.: ill. (Jahrbuch für Sozialökonomie und Gesellschaftstheorie).   H62.5.G4S78 1981
   Includes bibliographical references.

282

Teichler, Ulrich. Higher education and the labour market in the Federal Republic of Germany. Paris: International Institute for Educational Planning: Unesco Press, 1982. 178 p.   LC1085.T44 1982
   Includes bibliographical references.

283

Terry, W. Clinton. Teaching religion: the secularization of religion instruction in a West German school system. Washington, D. C.: University Press of America, 1981. xiv, 192 p.   LC410.G2T47
   Includes index.
   Bibliography: p. 177–187.

284

Vocational education in West Germany. [Edmonton, Alta.]: Alberta Education Planning & Research, 1981. 43, 14, 6 p.
   LC1047.G3V63

285

Vogt, Paul, 1926- Museum Folkwang Essen: die Geschichte einer Sammlung junger Kunst im Ruhrgebiet. Verb. und erw. Aufl. Köln: Dumont, 1983. 199 p.: ill. (some col.).   N2299.V6 1983
   Includes index.

286

Voices East and West: German short stories since 1945/ translations and introduction by Roger C. Norton. New York: F. Ungar Pub. Co., 1984.   PT1327.V65 1984
   Not presently in LC collections.

287

"—wird unser Reich Jahrtausend dauern'': Bielefeld 1933–1945: Kunst und Kunstpolitik im Nationalsozialismus: Kunsthalle Bielefeld, 10. September–25. Oktober 1981/ [Konzeption der Ausstellung und des Kataloges, R. Jörn]. Bielefeld: Die Kunsthalle, 1981. 36 p.: ill.
   N6868.5.N37W57 1981
   Exhibition catalog.

288

Wissenschaftshilfe für Entwicklungsländer/ [Herausgeber, Ministerium für Wissenschaft und Kunst, Baden-Württemberg, Presse- und Öffentlichkeitsreferat. Villingen-Schwenningen: Neckar-Verlag, 1982. ix, 114 p.: ill. (Bildung in neuer Sicht; n.f., Nr. 45)

LB5.B53 n.F., Nr. 45

Politics and Government

289

Die Andere deutsche Frage: Kultur und Gesellschaft der Bundesrepublik Deutschland nach dreissig Jahren/ herausgegeben von Walter Scheel. Stuttgart: Klett-Cotta, 1981. 344 p.   DD259.A754 1981
Includes index.

290

Armbruster, Frank. Politik in Deutschland: Systemvergleich Bundesrepublik Deutschland—DDR. Wiesbaden; Gabler, 1981. 227 p.: ill.   JN3971.A58A75
Includes index.

291

Arnold, Hans, 1923 (Aug. 14)– Auswärtige Kulturpolitik: e. Überblick aus dt. Sicht. München; Wien: Hanser, 1980. 173 p.

DD259.4.A727

English translation has title: Foreign cultural policy.

292

Auseinandersetzung mit dem Terrorismus, Möglichkeiten der politischen Bildungsarbeit: Bericht über ein Seminar für Träger der politischen Bildung/ veranstaltet vom Bundesministerium des Innern. Bonn: Das Bundesministerium, 1981. 229 p.   HV6433.G3A94 1981
Includes bibliographical references.

293

Ausländer in der Bundesrepublik Deutschland und in der Schweiz: Segregation und Integration: eine vergleichende Untersuchung/ [herausgegeben von] Hans-Joachim Hoffmann-Nowotny, Karl-Otto Hondrich. Frankfurt/Main; New York: Campus Verlag, 1982. 635 p.: ill.   DD258.5.A95 1982
Includes bibliographies.

294

Die Aussenpolitik der Bundesrepublik Deutschland/ [Herausgeber],

Helga Haftendorn, Lothar Wilker, Claudia Wörmann. Berlin: Wissenschaftlicher Autoren-Verlag (WAV), 1982. xiv, 594 p.

DD258.8.A94 1982

Includes documents.

Includes bibliographies.

295

Die Aussenpolitische Lage Deutschlands am Beginn der achtziger Jahre/ mit Beiträgen von Wilhelm Grewe . . . [et al.]. Berlin: Duncker & Humblot, 1982. 212 p. (Studien zur Deutschlandfrage; Bd. 5)

DD260.5.A94 1982

(Veröffentlichung/ Göttinger Arbeitskreis; Nr. 428)

Contributions based on papers previously presented at the annual meeting of the Göttinger Arbeitskreis, held in Mainz, Apr. 17 and 18, 1980.

Includes bibliographical references.

296

Bahr, Egon, 1922– Was wird aus den Deutschen?: Fragen und Antworten. Reinbek bei Hamburg: Rowohlt, 1982. 236 p.

DD259.4.B31684 1982

297

Balfour, Michael Leonard Graham, 1908– West Germany: a contemporary history. New York: St. Martin's Press, 1982. 307 p.: map.

DD259.B34 1982

Includes index.

Bibliography: p. 293–300.

298

Banerjee, Jyotirmoy, 1946– GDR and detente: Divided Germany and East-West relations: an outsider's perspective. Bonn: Forschungsinstitut der Deutschen Gesellschaft für Auswärtige Politik: Vertrieb, Europa Union Verlag, 1981. iii, 92 p. (Arbeitspapiere zur internationalen Politik, 13)   JX1393.D46B35

Includes bibliographical references.

299

Barkholdt, Bernhard. Ausländerproblem, eine Zeitbombe?: Entscheidung zur Jahrtausendwende. Berg am See: K. Vowinckel, 1981. 255 p.: ill.

DD259.2.B337 1981

Includes bibliographical references.

300

Beyme, Klaus von. The political system of the Federal Republic of Germany. Aldershot, Hants.: Gower, 1983. xiii, 209 p.

JN3971.A2B49 1983

Includes bibliographies and index.

301

Blumenwitz, Dieter. Die Ostverträge im Lichte des internationalen Vertragsrechts, insbesondere der Wiener Vertragsrechtskonvention. Bonn: Kulturstiftung der Deutschen Vertriebenen, 1982. 119 p.

JX696 1982a

Includes the texts of the Wiener Vertragsrechtskonvention in English and German and related documents.

Includes indexes.

Bibliography: p. 108–114.

302

Böpple, Arthur. Sozialpolitik in der BRD: Löcher im Netz d. sozialen Sicherung. Frankfurt am Main: Verlag Marxistische Blätter, 1980. 166 p. (Marxistische Taschenbücher: Reihe Marxismus aktuell; 146)

HD7179.B56

Includes bibliograpical references.

303

Bruns, Wilhelm, 1943– Deutsch-deutsche Beziehungen: Prämissen, Probleme, Perspektiven. 2., erw. und aktualisierte Aufl. Opladen: Leske und Budrich, 1979. 139 p. (Analysen; Bd. 23)

DD261.4.B767 1979

Bibliography: p. 117–121.

304

Bruns, Wilhelm, 1943– Die Uneinigen in den Vereinten Nationen: Bundesrepublik Deutschland und DDR in der UNO. Köln: Verlag Wissenschaft und Politik, 1980. 159, [1] p.: ill. (Bibliothek Wissenschaft und Politik; Bd. 25)

JX1977.2.G4B78

Bibliography: p. 157–160.

305

Bundesrepublik Deutschland und Deutsche Demokratische Republik: die beiden deutschen Staaten im Vergleich. Eckard Jesse (Hrsg.) Berlin: Colloquium Verlag, 1980. 415 p.

DD17.B86

Includes bibliographies.

306

Cappenberger Gespräch (17th: 1981: Düsseldorf, Germany) Bundeswehr,
Staat, Gesellschaft: ein Cappenberger Gespräch/ Referate von Franz-
Joseph Schulze und Carl-Gero von Ilsemann. Köln: Grote, 1981. 99 p.
DD259.4.C26 1981
Papers and discussions presented at the 17th Cappenberger Gespräch
of the Freiherr-vom-Stein-Gesellschaft held 1981 in Düsseldorf.

307

Childs, David, 1933– West Germany, politics and society. New York:
St. Martin's Press, 1981. 231 p.   JN3971.A5C46 1981
Includes bibliographies and indexes.

308

Comparative public policy and citizen participation: energy, education,
health and urban issues in the U. S. and Germany/ edited by Charles
R. Foster. New York: Pergamon Press, 1980. xv, 252 p.
JK1764.C65 1980
"Jointly sponsored by the Bonn University Center for Political Par-
ticipation and the Conference Group on German Politics."
Includes bibliographical references and index.

309

Conot, Robert E. Justice at Nuremberg. New York: Harper & Row,
1983. xiii, 593 p., [16] p. of plates: ill.   JX5437.8.C66 1983
Includes index.
Bibliography: p. 579–584.

310

Contemporary Germany: politics and culture/ edited by Charles Bur-
dick, Hans-Adolf Jacobsen, and Winfried Kudszus. Boulder, Colo.:
Westview Press, 1984.   DD259.4.C67 1984
Includes index.
Not presently in LC collections.

311

Czerwick, Edwin. Oppositionstheorien und Aussenpolitik: eine Analyse
sozialdemokratischer Deutschlandpolitik 1955 bis 1966. Königstein/Ts.:
Hain, 1981. 219 p. (Studien zum politischen System der Bundes-
republik Deutschland; Bd. 27)   DD259.4.C93 1981
Originally presented as the author's thesis (doctoral—Frankfurt am
Main, 1980) under the title: Die Deutschlandpolitik der SPD von 1955

bis 1966 unter besonderer Berücksichtigung ihrer Position als parlamentarische Oppositionspartei.
Includes index.
Bibliography: p. 199-213.

312
Deutsche Fragen, europäische Antworten/ herausgegeben von Ulrich Albrecht . . . [et al.]. Berlin: Verlag und Versandbuchhandlung Europäische Perspektiven, 1983. 222 p.   D1065.G3D48 1983
"Materialien zur 2. Europäischen Konferenz für Atomare Abrüstung"
Includes bibliographical references.

313
Dietze, Gottfried. Deutschland, wo bist Du?: suchende Gedanken aus Washington. Originalausg. München: G. Olzog, 1980. 160 p. (Geschichte und Staat; Bd. 240)   DD259.4.D54
Includes bibliographical references.

314
Dönhoff, Marion, Gräfin. Foe into friend: the makers of the new Germany from Konrad Adenauer to Helmut Schmidt. New York: St. Martin's Press, 1982. 214 p.   DD259.63.D6613 1982
Translation of: Von Gestern nach Übermorgen.
Includes bibliographical references and index.

315
Dönhoff, Marion, Gräfin. Von Gestern nach Übermorgen: zur Geschichte der Bundesrepublik Deutschland. Hamburg: A. Knaus, 1981. 317 p., [5] leaves of plates: ill.   DD259.D62 1981
Includes bibliographical references and index.

316
Doering-Manteuffel, Anselm. Die Bundesrepublik Deutschland in der Ära Adenauer: Aussenpolitik und innere Entwicklung, 1949-1963. Darmstadt: Wissenschaftliche Buchgesellschaft, 1983. x, 279 p.
DD259.D625 1983
Includes index.
Bibliography: p. 251-271.

317
Düwell, Kurt. Entstehung und Entwicklung der Bundesrepublik Deutschland (1945-1961): eine dokumentierte Einführung. Köln: Wien: Böhlau, 1981. xii, 403 p.   DD259.D83 1981
Includes bibliographical references and index.

318

Eisenmann, Peter, 1943- Aussenpolitik der Bundesrepublik Deutschland: von der Westintegration zur Verständigung mit dem Osten: ein Studienbuch. Krefeld: SINUS-Verlag, 1982. 232 p. (Gegenwart und Zeitgeschichte; Bd. 7) DD259.4.E39 1982
Includes index.
Bibliography: p. 167-171.

319

Emde, Heiner, 1931- Verrat und Spionage in Deutschland: Texte, Bilder, Dokumente. München: Ringier, 1980. 256 p.: ill. HV6275.E46
Bibliography: p. 255-256.

320

Engelmann, Bernt, 1921- Weissbuch, Frieden. Köln: Kiepenheuer & Witsch, 1982. 182 p. JX1963.E53 1982

321

Esser, Klaus. Key countries in the Third World: implications for relations between the Federal Republic of Germany and the South. Berlin: German Development Institute, 1981. xi, 204 p. (Occasional papers of the German Development Institute; no. 65). HC59.7.E78
Includes bibliographical references.

322

Facts about Germany: the Federal Republic of Germany. 3rd rev. ed. Gütersloh: Lexikothek Verlag, 1982. 414 p.: ill "Editorially closed 15 August 1981"— DD259.F32 1982
Includes index.

323

Federal Republic of Germany: a country study/ Foreign Area Studies, the American University; edited by Richard F. Nyrop. 2nd ed. [Washington, D. C.: American University, Foreign Area Studies]: For sale by the Supt. of Docs., U. S. G.P.O., 1982 (1983 printing) xxxii, 454 p.: ill. (Area handbook series). DD259.F43 1983
Rev. ed. of: Area handbook for the Federal Republic of Germany. 1975.
Includes index.
Bibliography: p. 399-433.

324

Feldman, Lily Gardner. The special relationship between West Germany and Israel. Boston: Allen & Unwin, 1984, c1983.
DD258.85.I75F45 1984
Not presently in LC collections.

325

Fetscher, Iring. Terrorismus und Reaktion in der Bundesrepublik Deutschland und in Italien. Reinbek bei Hamburg: Rowohlt, 1981. 218 p.   HV6433.G3F472
Bibliography: p. 182-196.

326

The Foreign policy of West Germany: formation and contents/ editors Ekkehart Krippendorff, Volker Rittberger. London; Beverly Hills: Sage, Publications, 1980. 372 p.: ill. (German political studies; v. 4)
                                JA55.G46 vol. 4
Includes bibliographical references.

327

Gastarbeiterpolitik oder Immigrationspolitik/ herausgegeben von Franz Ronneberger und Rudolf Vogel. München: Olzog, 1982. 202 p. (Südosteuropa-Studien; Heft 31)   HD8458.A2G365 1982
    Papers presented at a meeting organized by the Südosteuropa-Gesellschaft March 10-12, 1982, in Berlin.

328

Germany (West). Bundesministerium für Innerdeutsche Beziehungen. Auskünfte zum Stand der innerdeutschen Beziehungen, A-Z. 7., aktualisierte Aufl. Bonn: Der Bundesminister: Vertrieb, Gesamtdeutsches Institut, 1980. 104 p.   JX1549.Z7A2 1980a

329

Germany debates defense: the NATO Alliance at the crossroads/ edited by Rudolf Steinke and Michel Vale. Armonk, N. Y.: Published in collaboration with the Committee for a Nuclear-Free Europe [by] M. E. Sharpe, 1983. xxxii, 208 p.   UA710.G4613 1983
Includes bibliographical references.

330

Germany, keystone to European security: a symposium/ Peter Bender . . . [et al.]. Washington, D. C.: American Enterprise Institute for Public Policy Research, 1983. 71 p.   DD259.4.G39 1983
Includes bibliographical references.

331

Grabbe, Hans-Jürgen. Unionsparteien, Sozialdemokratie und Vereinigte Staaten von Amerika 1945-1966. Düsseldorf: Droste, 1983. 647 p.

(Beiträge zur Geschichte des Parlamentarismus und der politischen Parteien; Bd. 71)   DD259.4.G588 1983
Includes index.
Bibliography: p. 597-630.

332

Grebing, Helga. Die Nachkriegsentwicklung in Westdeutschland, 1945-1949. Stuttgart: Metzler, 1980. v. 1-2. (Studienreihe Politik; Bd. 7)   DD259.G59
Includes bibliographies.
Contents.—[Bd.] a. Die wirtschaftlichen Grundlagen.—[Bd.] b. Politik und Gesellschaft.

333

Gross, Johannes, 1932- Unsere letzten Jahre: Fragmente aus Deutschland 1970-1980. Stuttgart: Deutsche Verlags-Anstalt, 1980. 286 p.
     DD259.4.G753
Some articles originally published in the Frankfurter Allgemeine Zeitung and in Capital.

334

Die Grünen: Regierungspartner von Morgen? Jörg R. Mettke (Hg.) Reinbek bei Hamburg: Rowohlt, 1982. 270 p.
     JN3971.A98G72338 1982

335

Haffner, Sebastian. Überlegungen eines Wechselwählers. München: Kindler. 1980. 175 p.   JN3971.A979H27

336

Hamm-Brücher, Hildegard. Kulturbeziehungen weltweit: e. Werkstattbericht zur auswärtigen Kulturpolitik. München; Wien: Hanser, 1980. 226 p.   DD259.4.H228

337

Handbuch des deutschen Parteiensystems: Struktur und Politik in der Bundesrepublik zu Beginn der achtziger Jahre/ herausgegeben von Heino Kaack und Reinhold Roth. Opladen: Leske & Budrich, 1980. 2 v.   JN3971.A979H29
Includes indexes.
Bibliography: v. 1, p. 323-377; v. 2, p. 305-375.
Contents.—Bd. 1. Parteistrukturen und Legitimation des Parteiensystems — Bd. 2. Programmatik und politische Alternativen der Bundestagsparteien.

338

Handwörterbuch zur politischen Kultur der Bundesrepublik Deutschland: ein Lehr- und Nachschlagewerk/ Martin Greiffenhagen, Sylvia Greiffenhagen, Rainer Prätorius (Hrsg.). Opladen: Westdeutscher Verlag, 1981. 557 p. (Studienbücher zur Sozialwissenschaft; Bd. 45)

JA63.H23 1981

Includes bibliographies and indexes.

339

Hanrieder, Wolfram F. The foreign policies of West Germany, France, and Britain. Englewood Cliffs, N.J.: Prentice-Hall, 1980. xviii, 314 p.

DD259.4.H238

Includes index.
Bibliography: p. 297–299.

340

Hanson, Charles Goring. The closed shop: a comparative study in public policy and trade union security in Britain, the USA, and West Germany. New York: St. Martin's Press, 1981. 1982. x, 264 p.: map.

HD6488.2.G7H36 1982

Includes index.
Bibliography: p. 238–252.

341

Hartrich, Edwin. The Fourth and richest Reich. New York: Macmillan, 1980. xi, 302 p.: maps (on lining paper)   DD259.4.H35

Includes bibliographical references and index.

342

Herb, Hartmut. Der neue Rechtsextremismus: Fakten und Trends. Lohra-Rodenhausen: Winddruck Verlag, 1980. 194 p.: ill..

DD259.4.H4174

Bibliography: p. 188–190.

343

Heydemann, Günther, 1950– Geschichtswissenschaft im geteilten Deutschland: Entwicklungsgeschichte, Organisationsstruktur, Funktionen, Theorie- und Methodenprobleme in der Bundesrepublik Deutschland und in der DDR. Frankfurt a.M.; Bern; Cirencester/ U.K.: Lang, 1980. 267 p. (Erlanger historische Studien; Bd. 6)

DD86.H48 1980

Originally presented as the author's thesis (doctoral—Erlangen-Nürnberg).
Includes index.
Bibliography: p.251–266.

344

Hilfe + Handel = Frieden?: die Bundesrepublik in der Dritten Welt/
Redaktion Reiner Steinweg. Erstausg. Frankfurt am Main: Suhrkamp,
1982. 418 p.: ill. (Friedensanalysen; 15)   D888.G3H54 1982
Summaries in English.
Includes bibliographical references.

345

Holmes, Kim R. The West German peace movement and the national
question. Cambridge, Mass.: Institute for Foreign Policy Analysis,
1984. x, 76 p. (Foreign policy report) "February 1984."
                                              DD258.75.H65 1984
Includes bibliographical references.

346

Im Spannungsfeld der Weltpolitik, 30 Jahre deutsche Aussenpolitik
(1949–1979)/ Wolfram F. Hanrieder, Hans Rühle (Hrsg.). Stuttgart:
Bonn Aktuell, 1981. 359 p. (Studien zur Politik; Bd. 6)
                                              DD259.4.I45 1981
Contains papers presented at a conference held Jan. 4–6, 1979, spon-
sored by the University of California, Santa Barbara, and the Konrad-
Adenauer-Stiftung.
Includes bibliographical references.

347

Johnson, Nevil. State and government in the Federal Republic of Ger-
many: the executive at work. 2nd ed. Oxford [Oxfordshire]; New York:
Pergamon Press, 1983. x, 273 p.   JN3971.A55 1983
Rev. ed. of: Government in the Federal Republic of Germany. 1st
ed. 1973.
Includes index.
Bibliography: p. 267–268.

348

Jonas, Manfred. The United States and Germany: a diplomatic history.
Ithaca, N. Y.: Cornell University Press, 1984. 335 p.
                                              E183.8.G3J66 1984
Includes index.
Bibliography: p. 307–325.

349

Jühe, Reinhard, 1950– Gewerkschaften in der Bundesrepublik
Deutschland: Daten, Fakten, Strukturen. 2., aktualisierte und
erweiterte Aufl. Köln: Deutscher Instituts-Verlag, 1982. 288 p.: ill.
                                              HD6694.J83 1982
Includes index.

350

Kade, Gerhard. Die Amerikaner und wir. Köln: Pahl-Rugenstein, 1983.
139 p.   E183.8.G3K33 1983
Includes bibliographical references.

351

Kade, Gerhard. Die Russen und wir. Köln: Pahl-Rugenstein, 1983.
150 p.   DK67.5.G3K32 1983
Includes bibliographical references.

352

Kämpfen für die Sanfte Republik: Ausblicke auf die achtziger Jahre/
Freimut Duve, Heinrich Böll, Klaus Staeck (Hg.). Originalausg.
Reinbek bei Hamburg: Rowohlt, 1980. 189 p.   DD259.4.K24

353

Kanarowski, S. M. (Stanley M.) The German Army and NATO strategy.
Fort Lesley J. McNair, Washington, D. C.: National Defense University Press; Washington, D. C.: Supt. of Docs., U.S. G.P.O.,
[distributor], 1982. vi, 94 p.: 1 map. (National security affairs
monograph series; 82-2) "Research Directorate."
                                          UA712.K24 1982
Includes bibliographical references.

354

Keck, Otto. Policymaking in a nuclear program: the case of the West
German fast-breeder reactor. Lexington, Mass.: Lexington Books,
1981. xxvii, 274 p.: ill.   TK9203.B7K42
Based on the author's thesis, University of Sussex, 1977.
Includes bibliographical references and index.

355

Kershaw, Ian. Popular opinion and political dissent in the Third Reich,
Bavaria 1933-1945. Oxford, [Oxfordshire]; Clarendon Press; New
York: Oxford University Press, 1983. xii, 425 p.
                                          HN460.P8K47 1983
Includes index.
Bibliography: p. 398-411.

356

Kistler, Helmut. Die Ostpolitik der Bundesrepublik Deutschland,
1966-1973. Bonn: Bundeszentrale für Politische Bildung, 1982. 175 p.
                                          DD258.85.G35K57 1982
Bibliography: p. 174-175.

357

Köpper, Ernst-Dieter. Gewerkschaften und Aussenpolitik: die Stellung der westdeutschen Gewerkschaften zur wirtschaftlichen und militärischen Integration der Bundesrepublik in die Europäische Gemeinschaft und in die NATO. Frankfurt/Main; New York: Campus Verlag, 1982. viii, 445 p.　　　HD6490.F58K66 1982
Originally presented as the author's thesis (doctoral)—Universität Münster.
Bibliography: p. 418–445.

358

Kohn, Walter S. G. Governments and politics of the German-speaking countries. Chicago: Nelson-Hall, 1980.　　　JN3221.K58
Includes index.

359

Kolinsky, Eva. Parties, opposition, and society in West Germany. New York: St. Martin's Press; London: Croom Helm, 1984.
JN3971.A979K66 1984
Includes index.
Not presently in LC collections.

360

Krause, Christian L. From comparison of military capabilities to appraisal of the security situation: a study for the Friedrich-Ebert-Stiftung. 2nd rev. ed. Bonn: Study Group on Security and Disarmament in the Friedrich-Ebert-Stiftung, Research Institute, 1981. 45 leaves.
UB251.G4K7 1981
Includes bibliographical references.

361

Kühn, Heinz, 1912– Widerstand und Emigration: d. Jahre 1928–1945. Hamburg: Hoffmann und Campe, 1980. 357 p.
DD259.7.K83A34
Includes index.
Continued by: Aufbau und Bewährung. 1981.

362

Kulturarbeit, die Innenpolitik von morgen/ hrsg. von Rainer Silkenbeumer. Hannover: Fackelträger, 1980. 187 p.
DD259.25.K84 1980
Includes bibliographical references.

363

Kulturpolitisches Wörterbuch: Bundesrepublik Deutschland/Deutsche
Demokratische Republik im Vergleich/ herausgegeben von Wolfgang
R. Langenbucher, Ralf Rytlewski und Bernd Weyergraf. Stuttgart:
J. B. Metzler, 1983. 828 p.   DD259.K84 1983
   Includes indexes.
   Bibliography: p. 823–828.

364

Lampert, Heinz. Sozialpolitik. Berlin; Heidelberg; New York: Springer,
1980. xxi, 519 p.: ill.   HN17.5.L32
   Includes indexes.
   Bibliography: p. 500–509.

365

Lehmann, Hans Georg. Chronik der Bundesrepublik Deutschland
1945/49–1981. München: Beck, 1981. 209 p.   DD259.L43
   Includes index.
   Bibliography: p. 186–195.

366

Leinemann, Jürgen. Die Angst der Deutschen: Beobachtungen zur
Bewusstseinslage der Nation. Hamburg: Rowohlt Taschenbuch Verlag,
1982. 191 p.   DD259.L44 1982

367

Die Linke und die nationale Frage: Dokumente zur deutschen Einheit
seit 1945/ hrsg. von Peter Brandt und Herbert Ammon. Orig.-Ausg.
Reinbek bei Hamburg: Rowohlt, 1981. 379 p.   DD257.4.L53
   Includes index.
   Bibliography: p. 367–371.

368

Mendershausen, Horst. The defense of Germany and the German defense
contribution. Santa Monica, Calif.: Rand Corp., 1981. iii, 26 p.
                      AS36.R28 no. 6686
   Includes bibliographical references.

369

Merkl, Peter H. The origin of the West German Republic. Westport,
Conn.: Greenwood Press, 1982, 1963. xviii, 269 p.: map.
                      JN3971.A2M47 1982

Reprint. Originally published: New York: Oxford University Press, 1963.
Includes index.
Bibliography: p. 249–264.

370
Militarismus in der Bundesrepublik: Ursachen und Formen/ Heinz Becker, Otmar Leist (Hrsg.); in Zusammenarbeit mit der Deutschen Friedensgesellschaft, Vereinigte Kriegsdienstgegner, Gruppe Bremen. Köln: Pahl-Rugenstein, 1981. 140 p.: ill.　　　　UA710.M529
Includes bibliographies.

371
Die Moderne deutsche Geschichte in der internationalen Forschung: 1945–1975/ hrsg. von Hans-Ulrich Wehler. Göttingen: Vandenhoeck und Ruprecht, 1978. 286 p. (Geschichte und Gesellschaft: Sonderheft; 4)　　　　DD203.M62
Includes bibliographical references.

372
Müller-Roschach, Herbert. Die deutsche Europapolitik 1949–1977: e. politische Chronik. Bonn: Europa Union Verlag, 1980. 467 p. (Europäische Schriften des Instituts für Europäische Politik: Bd. 55)　　　　DD411.B5 Bd. 55
Includes bibliographical references and indexes.

373
Nelkin, Dorothy. The atom besieged: extraparliamentary dissent in France and Germany. Cambridge, Mass.: MIT Press, 1981. x, 235 p.: ill.　　　　HD9698.F72N44
Includes bibliographical references and index.

374
Der Neue Realismus: Aussenpolitik nach Iran u. Afghanistan/ hrsg. von Helmut Kohl. Düsseldorf: Erb, 1980. 230 p.　　　　D849.N48
Rev. papers of a meeting held by the Christlich-Demokratische Union, March 4–5, 1980.

375
Neutralität, eine Alternative?: zur Militär- und Sicherheitspolitik neutraler Staaten in Europa/ Dieter S. Lutz, Annemarie Grosse-Jütte (Hrsg.). Baden-Baden: Nomos Verlagsgesellschaft, 1982. 279 p.: ill. (Militär, Rüstung, Sicherheit; Bd. 4)　　　　UA646.N47 1982
Includes bibliographical references.

376

Noack, Paul. Die Aussenpolitik der Bundesrepublik Deutschland. 2., überarb. und erw. Aufl. Stuttgart; Berlin; Köln; Mainz: Kohlhammer, 1981. 216 p.   DD257.4.N58 1981
First ed. published in 1972 under title: Deutsche Aussenpolitik seit 1945.
Includes index.
Bibliography: p. 202-214.

377

Ockenfels, Winfried. Signale in die achtziger Jahre: d. politische Landschaft d. Bundesrepublik Deutschland: Zahlen, Daten, Fakten, Meinungen. München; Wien: Olzog, 1980. 232 p.: ill. (Geschichte und Staat; Bd. 238/239)   DD259.4.O25
Includes bibliographical references.

378

Olzog, Günter, 1919- Die politischen Parteien in der Bundesrepublik Deutschland: mit Text des Parteigesetzes. 12., überarb. Aufl. München; Wien: Olzog, 1980. 192 p. (Geschichte und Staat; Bd. 104)
JN3971.A979O4 1980
Bibliography: p. 190-192.

379

Papadakis, Elim. The Green Movement in West Germany. London: Croom Helm; New York: St. Martin's Press, 1984. 230 p.
JN3971.A98G7236 1984
Includes index.
Bibliography: 221-226.

380

Pauly, Wolfgang, 1949- Christliche Demokraten und Christlich-Soziale: Untersuchung zum interparteilichen Bündnisverhalten von CDU und CSU, 1969-1979. Trier: [s.n.], 1981. 503 p.
JN3971.A98C4563 1981
Thesis (doctoral)—Universität Trier, 1981.
Bibliography: p. 449-503.

381

The Political economy of West Germany: Modell Deutschland/ edited by Andrei S. Markovits. New York: Praeger Publishers, 1982. xiv, 238 p.   HC286.5.P624 1982
Includes index.
Bibliography: p. 225-228.

382

Politik für die 80er [i.e. achtziger] Jahre: was steht zur Wahl?/ mit Beitr.
von Willy Brandt . . . [et al.].; hrsg. von Peter Juling. Gerlingen:
Bleicher, 1980. 279 p.   JN3971.A979P58
    Includes index.
    Bibliography: p. 273-274.

383

Politische Zeittafel 1949-1979: drei Jahrzehnte Bundesrepublik
Deutschland/ Hans Ulrich Behn. Erhardt Eisenacher. 2. Aufl. Bonn:
Presse- und Informationsamt der Bundesregierung, 1981. 401 p.
                                                  DD259.4.P648 1981
    Includes index.
    Bibliography: p. 287-336.

384

Probst, Ulrich. The Communist parties in the Federal Republic of Germany. Frankfurt/Main: Haag + Herchen, 1981. ii, 130 p.
                                  JN3971.A979P75613 1981
    Translation of: Die kommunistischen Parteien der Bundesrepublik
Deutschland.
    Includes index.
    Bibliography: p. 81-112.

385

Pross, Harry, 1923- Politik und Publizistik in Deutschland seit 1945:
zeitbedingte Positionen. München: R. Piper, 1980. 268 p.
                                    PN5214.P6P76
    Contains 17 essays, 16 of which were previously published in various
sources, 1952-1979.
    Includes bibliographical references.

386

Raach, Jörg, 1950- Politische Bildung zwischen kaltem Krieg und Ent-
spannung: Voraussetzungen und Erfordernisse von Ost-West-
Bildungsarbeit, Bestandsaufnahme ihrer Praxis in der politischen
Erwachsenenbildung. Frankfurt am Main; Bern: Lang, 1981. 266 p.
(Europäische Hochschulschriften. Reihe XI, Pädagogik; Bd. 114).
                                    D843.R2 1981
    Bibliography: p. 240-263.

387

Rasch, Harold. NATO-Bündnis oder Neutralität?: Plädoyer für eine neue
Aussenpolitik. Köln: Pahl-Rugenstein, 1981. 138 p.
                                    UA646.5.G4R37 1981

"Verzeichnis der wichtigsten Veröffentlichungen von Professor Dr. Harold Rasch": p. 137– 138.
Includes bibliographical references.

388

Rausch, Heinz Volker. Politische Kultur in der Bundesrepublik Deutschland. Berlin: Colloquium Verlag, 1980. 107 p. (Beiträge zur Zeitgeschichte; Bd. 1)　　　　　JN3971.A91R38
Bibliography: p. 104–107.

389

The Relations between the People's Republic of China and I. Federal Republic of Germany, II. German Democratic Republic in 1981 as seen by Xinhua News Agency: a documentation/ compiled by Wolfgang Bartke. Hamburg: Institute of Asian Affairs, 1982. 291 p.
DD258.85.C6R45 1982

390

Report on domestic and international terrorism/ Subcommittee on Civil and Constitutional Rights of the Committee on the Judiciary, Ninety-seventh Congress, first session. Washington: U. S. G.P.O., 1981. v, 36 p.　　　　　HV6433.G3R46
"April 1981."

391

Richter, Peter. Schwerpunktland Mexiko: zur Fortentwicklung der bilateralen Kooperationspolitik der Bundesrepublik Deutschland. Berlin: Deutsches Institut für Entwicklungspolitik, 1981. iv, 110 p. (Schriften des Deutschen Instituts für Entwicklungspolitik (DIE); Bd. 67)　　　　　HF1546.15.M6R52 1981
　　Includes texts of 1981 economic agreements between France and Mexico (in Spanish), and West Germany and Iraq.
Bibliography: p. 80–86.

392

Rupp, Hans Karl. Politische Geschichte der Bundesrepublik Deutschland: Entstehung und Entwicklung; eine Einführung. 2. erw. und verb. Aufl. Stuttgart: W. Kohlhammer, 1982, 1978. 242 p.
DD258.75.R87 1982
　　Includes index.
Bibliography: p. 210–222.

393

Schmidt, Helmut, 1918 Dec. 23– Helmut Schmidt, perspectives on politics/ edited by Wolfram F. Hanrieder. Boulder, Colo.: Westview

Press, 1982. vi, 247 p.: ports.   DD259.7.S36A5 1982
Includes index.
Bibliography: p. 237-238.

394

Schmollinger, Horst W. Zwischenbilanz: 10 Jahre sozialliberale Politik
1969-1979: Anspruch und Wirklichkeit. Hannover: Fackelträger, 1980.
230 p.   JN3971.A91S36
Bibliography: p. 227-230.

395

Schneider, Eberhard, 1941- Der Nationsbegriff der DDR und seine
deutschlandpolitische Bedeutung. Köln: Bundesinstitut für Ostwissenschaftliche und Internationale Studien, 1981. iii, 25 p. (Berichte des
Bundesinstituts für Ostwissenschaftliche und Internationale Studien;
33-1981)   HX15.G468 1981-33
Summary in English and German.
Includes bibliographical references.

396

Schulz, Brigitte. Aid or imperialism? West Germany in Sub-Sahara
Africa. Boston, Mass. (115 Bay State Rd., Boston 02215): African
Studies Center, Boston University, 1982. 31 leaves. (Working papers/
African Studies Center; no. 61)   HF1546.15.A357S38 1982
Includes bibliographical references.

397

Schulz, Eberhard, 1926 Aug. 17- Die deutsche Nation in Europa: internationale und historische Dimensionen. Bonn: Europa Union, 1982.
272 p. (Schriften des Forschungsinstituts der Deutschen Gesellschaft
für Auswärtige Politik e.V.)   DD120.E8S38 1982
Includes index.
Bibliography: p. 255-261.

398

Schweigler, Gebhard, 1943- West German foreign policy: the domestic
setting. New York, N.Y.: Praeger, 1984.   DD260.5.S39 1984
"Published with the Center for Strategic and International Studies,
Georgetown University, Washington, D. C."
Includes bibliographical references.
Not presently in LC collections.

399

Seidelmann, Reimund. Die Entspannungspolitik der Bundesrepublik
Deutschland: Entstehungsursachen, Konzepte und Perspektiven.

Frankfurt/Main; New York: Campus, 1982. 194 p.

DD259.4.S416 1982

Bibliography: p. 192–194.

400

Smith, Gordon R. Democracy in Western Germany: parties and politics in the Federal Republic. 2nd ed. London: Heinemann, 1982. ix, 229 p.: ill., maps.   JN3971.A979S55

Includes bibliographies and index.

401

Smyser, W. R., 1931– German-American relations. Beverly Hills: Sage Publications, 1980. 88 p. (The Washington papers; v. VIII, 74)

E183.8.G3S58

Bibliography: p. 85–88.

402

Soziale Kulturarbeit: Berichte und Analysen/ herausgegeben von Armin Fuchs und Heinz-Wilhelm Schnieders. Weinheim: Beltz, 1982. 207 p.: ill.   DD259.25.S69 1982

Bibliography: p. 196–206.

403

Stand und Zukunft der deutsch-arabischen Beziehungen: Beiträge und Diskussion einer Konferenz vom 19. Februar 1981 in Bonn/ Forschungsinstitut der Deutschen Gesellschaft für Auswärtige Politik e.V. Bonn: Das Institut: Vertrieb, Europa Union Verlag, 1981. i, 57 p. (Arbeitspapiere zur internationalen Politik, 15)   DS63.2.G4S74

404

Studies in comparative federalism: West Germany: an information report. Washington, D. C.: Advisory Commission on Intergovernmental Relations: [For sale by the Supt. of Docs., U. S. G.P.O.], 1981. x, 89 p.: ill.

HJ1120.S85

"July 1981."

Bibliography: p. 81–89.

405

Vademecum der Auslandskulturarbeit: Informationen über die Tätigkeit amtlicher Stellen, Mittlerorganisationen und Institutionen in der auswärtigen Kulturarbeit/ bearbeitet und zusammengestellt von Heino Lederer im Auftrag des Auswärtigen Amtes, Abteilung für Auswärtige Kulturpolitik. 2. Aufl.,/ Stand Dezember 1980 bearbeitet und erw.

von Ruth Ziervogel-Tamm. Stuttgart: Institut für Auslandsbeziehungen, 1981?, 121 p.   DD68.V33 1981
    Bibliography: p. 121.

406

Weidenfeld, Werner. Die Frage nach der Einheit der deutschen Nation.
München: G. Olzog, 1981. 154 p.   DD257.4.W36 1981
    Includes index.
    Bibliography: p. 141-152.

407

West German foreign policy: dilemmas and directions/ edited by Peter
H. Merkl. Chicago, Ill. (116 South Michigan Ave., Chicago 60603):
Chicago Council on Foreign Relations, 1982. 190 p. Contains essays
from a project sponsored by the Chicago Council on Foreign Relations in cooperation with the Konrad Adenauer Foundation.
                                              DD258.8.W47 1982
    Includes bibliographical references.

408

Wettig, Gerhard. Die Friedensbewegung der beginnenden 80er Jahre.
Köln: Bundesinstitut für Ostwissenschaftliche und Internationale Studien, 1982. ii, 26 p. (Berichte des Bundesinstituts für Ostwissenschaftliche und Internationale Studien; 9-1982)   HX15.G468 1982-9
    Summary in English and German.
    Includes bibliographical references.

409

Wettig, Gerhard. The relations of the USSR with the Federal Republic
of Germany. Köln, Federal Republic of Germany: Federal Institute
for East European and International Studies, 1982. iii, 37 p. (Berichte
des Bundesinstituts für Ostwissenschaftliche und Internationale Studien; 12-1982)   HX15.G468 1982-12
    Includes bibliographical references.

410

Wettig, Gerhard. The role of West Germany in Soviet policies toward
Western Europe. Köln: Bundesinstitut für Ostwissenschaftliche und
Internationale Studien, 1982. 25 p.   DK67.5.G3W396 1982.
    Includes bibliographical references.

411

Zimmermann, Ulrich, 1936- Geliebt, verkannt und doch geachtet: Franz
Josef Strauss, der Mensch, der Politiker, der Staatsmann von A-Z.

2. Aufl. Percha am Starnberger See: R. S. Schulz, 1980. 237 p.
DD259.7.S7Z55 1980.

Religion

412

Abdullah, Muhammad S., 1931– Geschichte des Islams in Deutschland.
Graz; Wien; Köln: Styria, 1981. 220 p. (Islam und westliche Welt;
Bd. 5)   BP65.G3A219
Includes index.
Bibliography: p. 206–217.

413

Hach, Jürgen. Gesellschaft und Religion in der Bundesrepublik
Deutschland: e. Einf. in d. Religionssoziologie. Heidelberg: Quelle und
Meyer, 1980. 217 p. (Uni-Taschenbücher; Bd. 997)
BR856.3.H28
Includes bibliographies and indexes.

414

Juden, Judentum und Staat Israel im christlichen Religionsunterricht in
der Bundesrepublik Deutschland: Unters. im Rahmen d.
Forschungsschwerpunkts ''Geschichte u. Religion d. Judentums'' an
d. Univ. Duisburg, Gesamthochsch./ Herbert Jochum, Heinz Kremers
(Hrsg.). Paderborn; München; Wien; Zürich: Schöningh, 1980. 191 p.
BM535.J837
Bibliography: p. 155–180.

415

Sladden, John Cyril. Boniface of Devon: apostle of Germany. Exeter
[Eng]: Paternoster Press, 1980. 254 p.: maps (on lining papers).
BX4700.B7S56
Includes index.
Bibliography: p. 237–238.

416

Zur Religionsgeschichte der Bundesrepublik Deutschland/ Günter Kehrer
(Hrsg.). München: Kösel, 1980. 199 p. (Forum Religionswissenschaft;
Bd. 2)   BL860.Z87
Includes bibliographies and index.

Society

417

Bellebaum, Alfred. Soziologie der modernen Gesellschaft. 3. neubearb. Aufl. Hamburg: Hoffmann und Campe, 1980. 319 p. (Kritische Wissenschaft)   HM57.B396 1980
   Includes indexes.
   Bibliography: p. 287–306.

418

Böddeker, Günter. Die Flüchtlinge: die Vertreibung der Deutschen im Osten. München: F. Herbig, 1980. 383 p., [35] leaves of plates: ill.
                                                D809.G3B63
   Includes index.
   Bibliography: p. 374–377.

419

Brauchtum der Heimat: von Deutschen aus dem Osten bewahrt und weitergegeben/ Hans-Ulrich Engel (Hrsg.). Stuttgart: H. Poller, 1983. 149 p.: 1 ill. Prepared for a series of broadcasts by the Bayerischer Rundfunk.   GT4850.A2B68 1983
   Includes index.

420

Cramer, Alfons. Zur Lage der Familie und der Familienpolitik in der Bundesrepublik Deutschland. Opladen: Leske + Budrich, 1982. 179 p.: ill. (Forschungstexte Wirtschafts- und Sozialwissenschaften; Bd. 7)   HQ626.C7 1982
   A revision of the author's Habilitationsschrift, 1980.
   Bibliography: p. 170–179.

421

Dralle, Lothar. Slaven an Havel und Spree: Studien zur Geschichte des hevellisch-wilzischen Fürstentums (6. bis 10. Jahrhundert). Berlin: In Kommission bei Duncker & Humblot, 1981. 336 p., [3] p. of plates: 4 maps. (Osteuropastudien der Hochschulen des Landes Hessen. Reihe 1, Giessener Abhandlungen zur Agrar- und Wirtschaftsforschung des europäischen Ostens, Bd. 108)   DJK27.D7 1981
   The author's Habilitationsschrift, Justus-Liebig-Universität Giessen, 1979.
   Summary in English.

422

Frauenemanzipation und berufliche Bildung: Programme, Bildungs-konzepte, Erfahrungsberichte/ Marianne Weg, Angela Jurinek-Stinner

(Hg.). München: Hueber, 1982. 187 p.: ill.   HQ1625.F69 1982
(Erwachsenenbildung und Gesellschaft)
Bibliography: p. 171–182.

423

Eine Generation später: Bundesrepublik Deutschland 1953–1979/ Institut
für Demoskopie Allensbach; Elisabeth Noelle-Neumann und Edgar Piel
(Hrsg.). München; New York: Saur, 1983. 272 p. Pt. 1 includes papers
from a meeting held May 20, 1981 in Bonn.
                                              HN445.5.G384 1983
Includes bibliographical references.

424

German feminism: readings in politics and literature/ edited by Edith
Hoshino Altbach . . . [et al.]. Albany, N.Y.: State University of New
York Press, 1984. xii, 389 p.   HQ1625.G465 1984
Includes bibliographies and index.

425

Kühn, Horst. Bürgerliche Psychologie in der BRD. Berlin: Volk und
Wissen, 1980. 208 p. (Beiträge zur Psychologie; Bd. 8)
                                              BF108.G3K83
Bibliography: p. 196–208.

426

Neumann, Lothar F. Die Sozialordnung der Bundesrepublik Deutschland. Frankfurt; New York: Campus Verlag, 1982. 142 p.: ill.
                                              HN445.5.N46 1982
Bibliography: p. 140–142.

427

Pöggeler, Franz. Menschenführung in der Bundeswehr: Ausbildung der
Vorgesetzten in der Bundeswehr auf dem Gebiet der Menschenführung. Bonn: Bundesministerium der Verteidigung, 1980. 207 p.:
ill. (Schriftenreihe Innere Führung, Heft Nr. 1/1980)   UB210.P55
Bibliography: p. 200–206.

428

Population change and social planning: social and economic implications
of the recent decline in fertility in the United Kingdom and the Federal
Republic of Germany/ edited by David Eversley and Wolfgang
Köllmann. London: Arnold, 1982. ix, 485 p.: ill.
                                              HB3583.P598 1982
Includes index.
Bibliography: p. 411–446.

429

Sauerzapf, Maria. Das Krankenhauswesen in der Bundesrepublik
Deutschland: institutionelle Regelungen aus ökonomischer Sicht.
Baden-Baden: Nomos-Verlagsgesellschaft, 1980. 176 p. (Wirtschafts-
recht und Wirtschaftspolitik; Bd. 65)   RA989.G3S28
Bibliography: p. 167–175.

430

Schepping, Johanna. Christlich orientierte Sozialerziehung. Donauwörth:
Auer, 1981. 189 p.: ill.   LC431.G3S26 1981
Bibliography: p. 179–189.

431

Schütt, Peter, 1939– "Der Mohr hat seine Schuldigkeit getan—": gibt
es Rassismus in der Bundesrepublik?: eine Streitschrift. Dortmund:
Weltkreis-Verlag, 1981. 263 p.: ill.   DD74.S34
Bibliography: p. 263.

432

Shaffer, Harry G. Women in the two Germanies: a comparative study
of a socialist and a non-socialist society. New York: Pergamon Press,
1981. xvi, 235 p.   HQ1630.5.S52 1981
Includes index.
Bibliography: p. 211–225.

433

Simon, Ulrich. Die Integration der Bundeswehr in die Gesellschaft: d.
Ringen um d. innere Führung. Heidelberg; Hamburg: v. Decker,
1980. xxv, 411 p.   UA710.S517
Includes index.
Bibliography: p. 376–404.

434

Sozialstruktur der Bundesrepublik Deutschland/ bearbeitet von Gerhard
Kappl. Bamberg: Buchner, 1980 (1982 printing) 119 p.: ill. (some col.)
(Arbeitstexte Politik; Bd. 1)   HM131.S6189 1982
Bibliography: p. 119.

435

Vom Gastarbeiter zum Bürger: Ausländer in der Bundesrepublik
Deutschland herausgegeben von Wilfried Röhrich. Berlin: Duncker
& Humblot, 1982. 94 p. (Beiträge zur Sozialforschung; Bd. 2)
          HD8458.A2V64 1982
Includes bibliographical references.

436

Wild, Martin Trevor, 1940– West Germany, a geography of its people. Totowa, N.J.: Barnes & Noble Books, 1980. 1979. 255 p.: ill.

GF576.W54 1980

Includes index.
Bibliography: p. 230–243.

GERMAN DEMOCRATIC REPUBLIC

Bibliography and Reference Works

437

Bibliographie wissenschaftlicher Arbeiten. Jena [Ger.] Friedrich-Schiller-Universität Jena, 1979. 237 p. Z7403.B598 1979

438

Bibliographie zur Deutschlandpolitik 1941–1974/ hrsg. vom Bundesministerium für Innerdeutsche Beziehungen. Frankfurt am Main: A. Metzner, 1975. 248 p. Z2240.3.B5
(Dokumente zur Deutschlandpolitik: Beihefte; Bd. 1)
Includes index.

439

Buch, Günther. Namen und Daten wichtiger Personen der DDR/ 3., überarbeitete und erw. Aufl. Berlin: Dietz, 1982. xv, 384 p.

CT1099.2.B82 1982

440

Edgington, Peter William. The politics of the two Germanies: a guide to sources and English-language materials. Ormskirk: G. W. and A. Hesketh, 1977. xiv, 80 p. Z2221.E33

441

Gerber, Margy. Literature of the German Democratic Republic in English translation: a bibliography: studies in GDR culture and society: a supplementary volume. Lanham, MD, University Press of America, 1984. Z2250.G45 1984

442

Haupt, Michael. Die Berliner Mauer: Vorgeschichte, Bau, Folgen: Literaturbericht und Bibliographie zum 20. Jahrestag des 13. August 1961. München: Bernard & Graefe, 1981. ix, 230 p.

Z2244.B5H29

(Schriften der Bibliothek für Zeitgeschichte; Bd. 21)
Includes bibliographical references and index.

443

Hundegger, Helga. Dissertationen und Habilitationen auf dem Gebiet
der Deutschlandforschung, 1969–1978: Hochschulschriften aus der
Deutschen Demokratischen Republik und Berlin (Ost). Bonn: Gesamtdeutsches Institut, 1980. xxii, 103 p.   Z2221.H86 1980
Includes index.

444

Künstler der DDR. Dresden: Verlag der Kunst, 1981. 343 p.: ill. (some
col.)   N6889.4.K86 1981
Includes index.
Bibliography: p. 337–339.

445

Kulturpolitisches Wörterbuch: Bundesrepublik Deutschland/Deutsche
Demokratische Republik im Vergleich/herausgegeben von Wolfgang
R. Langenbucher, Ralf Rytlewski und Bernd Weyergraf. Stuttgart:
J. B. Metzler, 1983. 828 p.   DD259.K84 1983
Includes index.
Bibliography: p. 823–828.

446

Merritt, Anna J. Politics, economics, and society in the two Germanies,
1945–75: a bibliography of English-language works. Urbana: University of Illinois Press, 1978. xix, 268 p.   Z7165.G3M47
Includes index.

447

Tautz, Günter. Orden, Preise und Medaillen: staatliche Auszeichnungen
der Deutschen Demokratischen Republik. Leipzig: Bibliographisches
Institut, 1980. 198 p.   CR5109.T38 1980

448

Totok, Wilhelm. Handbuch der bibliographischen Nachschlagewerke.
6., erw. völlig neu bearbeitete Aufl. Frankfurt am Main: Klostermann,
1984.   Z1002.T68 1984
Includes index.
Table of contents and ''Bibliographische Terminologie'' in English,
French, and German.

449

Ullmann, Hans-Peter. Bibliographie zur Geschichte der deutschen Parteien und Interessenverbände. Göttingen: Vandenhoeck und Ruprecht, 1978. 263 p. (Arbeitsbücher zur modernen Geschichte; Bd. 6)   Z7165.G3U44

450

United States. Central Intelligence Agency. National Foreign Assessment Center. Directory of officials of the German Democratic Republic. Washington, D. C.: The Center, 1980. x, 267 p.
                                                    JN3971.5.A4U54 1980
"Information received as of 23 November 1979 has been used in preparing this directory."

Description and Travel

451

East Germany: a country study/ Foreign Area Studies, the American University: edited by Eugene K. Keefe. 2nd ed. Washington, D. C.: American University, Foreign Area Studies: For sale by the Supt. of Docs., U. S. G.P.O., 1982. xxxi, 348 p.: ill.   DD261.E27 1982
"Research completed July 1981."
Includes index.
Bibliography: p. 313–327.

452

Reiseatlas mit 60 Autorouten durch die DDR. Berlin: VEB Tourist Verlag, 1981. xviii, 25, 193 p.: ill., col. maps.   DD16.R38
Maps on lining papers.
Includes index.

453

Sperling, Walter. Landeskunde DDR: e. annotierte Auswahlbibliographie. München; New York: Verlag Dokumentation, 1978. xxii, 456 p.   Z2250.S64
(Bibliographien zur regionalen Geographie und Landeskunde; Bd. 1) Includes indexes.

Economy

454

Bryson, Phillip J. The consumer and socialist planning: the East German case. New York, Praeger, 1984.   HC290.795.C6B79 1984
Includes index.

455

Bundesrepublik Deutschland—DDR, die Wirtschaftssysteme: soziale
Marktwirtschaft und sozialistische Planwirtschaft im Systemvergleich/
mit Beiträgen von Hannelore Hamel . . . et al. 4., überarbeitete und
erw. Aufl. München, C. H. Beck, 1983. 430 p.: ill.

HC286.5.B845 1983

Includes bibliographical references.

456

Haase, Herwig, 1945– Entwicklungstendenzen der DDR-Wirtschaft für
die 80er Jahre: eine Prognose der Probleme. Berlin: Osteuropa-Institut,
1980. 115 p.   HC244.A1B4 Nr. 40
(Wirtschaftswissenschaftliche Folge der Berichte des Osteuropa-
Instituts an der Freien Universität Berlin, Nr. 40)
(Berichte des Osteuropa-Instituts an der Freien Universität Berlin;
Heft 124. Reihe Wirtschaft und Recht)
Summary in English and German.
Includes index.
Bibliography: p. 111–114.

457

Leptin, Gert, 1929– Deutsche Wirtschaft nach 1945: ein Ost-West-
Vergleich. Opladen: Leske + Budrich, 1980. 85 p.

HC286.5.L49 1980

Includes index.
Bibliography: p. 81–82.

458

Thalheim, Karl Christian, 1900– Die wirtschaftliche Entwicklung der
beiden Staaten in Deutschland: Tatsachen und Zahlen. 2.,
überarbeitete und erg. Aufl. Berlin: Landeszentrale für Politische
Bildungsarbeit, 1981. 142 p.: col. ill.   HC286.5.T48 1981
Bibliography: p. 133–135.

459

Die Volkswirtschaft der DDR/ Autorenkollektiv, Günter Nötzold . . . [et
al]. Leipzig VEB Verlag Enzyklopädie, 1980. 156 p.: ill.

HC290.78.V62 1980

(Landeskunde DDR für Ausländer)
Includes bibliographical references.

460

Das Wirtschaftssystem der DDR: wirtschaftspolitische Gestaltungs-
probleme/ herausgegeben von Gernot Gutmann. Stuttgart; New York:

G. Fischer, 1983. ix, 461 p.: ill.   HC290.78.W57 1983
(Schriften zum Vergleich von Wirtschaftsordnungen; Heft 30)
Revised papers previously presented at a conference sponsored by
the Forschungsseminar Radein e.V. in 1981
Includes bibliographies and indexes.

Intellectual and Cultural Life

461

Bellut, Thomas. Die DDR-Berichterstattung in den Nachrichtenmedien
der Bundesrepublik Deutschland, Münster: Lit. Verlag, 1983. v, v,
316 p. ill.   PN5214.F67B45 1983
Bibliography: p. 304-316.

462

Bildung, Wissenschaft und kulturelles Leben in der DDR/ Autorenkollektiv Dieter Aner . . . [et al]. Leipzig: Verlag Enzyklopädie, 1981.
228 p.: ill.   DD261.2.B49 1981
(Landeskunde DDR für Ausländer)

463

Bildungsreformen in der Bundesrepublik Deutschland und in der
Deutschen Demokratischen Republik: Ergebnisse und Probleme
vergleichender Untersuchungen/ herausgegeben von Siegfried Baske;
mit Beiträgen von Oskar Anweiler . . . [et al.]. Heidelberg: Meyn,
1981. 200 p.   LC93.G42B52
(Schriftenreihe der Gesellschaft für Deutschlandforschung e.V.,
Berlin; Bd. 3)
Includes bibliographical references.

464

Buxhoeveden, Christina von, 1943- Geschichtswissenschaft und Politik
in der DDR: das Problem der Periodisierung. Köln: Verlag
Wissenschaft und Politik, 1980. 301, [1] p.   DD238.B87 1980
Originally presented as the author's thesis (doctoral—Friedrich-
Alexander-Universität Erlangen-Nürnberg, 1979) under the title:
Periodisierung als Problem für Politik und Geschichtswissenschaft in
der DDR.
Bibliography: p. 287-302.

465

Christliche Kunst im Kulturerbe der Deutschen Demokratischen
Republik. Kirchen, Klöster und ihre Kunstschätze in der DDR/ [Gerd

Baier . . . et al.]. München: Beck, 1982. 406, [1] p.: ill. (some col.)
NA1089.C48 1982
Originally published as: Christliche Kunst im Kulturerbe der
Deutschen Demokratischen Republik. Berlin: Union Verlag (VOB),
1982.
Bibliography: p. 407.

466

Clyne, Michael G., 1939– Language and society in the German-speaking
countries. Cambridge [Cambridgeshire]: New York: Cambridge
University Press, 1984.   PF3973.C55 1984
Includes indexes.

467

Conrad, Gabriele. Kind und Erzieher in der BRD und in der DDR.
Würzburg: Königshausen + Neumann, 1982. 487 p.: ill. (Interna-
tionale Pädagogik; Bd. 2)   LB1342.C66 1982
Originally presented as the author's thesis (doctoral).
Bibliography: p. 437–487.

468

Darsteller und Darstellungskunst: in Theater, Film, Fernsehen und Hör-
funk/ herausgegeben von Ernst Schumacher. Berlin: Henschelverlag
Kunst und Gesellschaft, 1981. 459 p.   PN2654.D34 1981
(Schriftenreihe des Lehrstuhls Theorie der Darstellenden Künste im
Bereich Theaterwissenschaft der Sektion Ästhetik und Kunstwissen-
schaften der Humboldt-Universität Berlin; Bd. 1).
Includes bibliographical references.

469

Dvoracek, Rolf. Festtage in Bautzen: Bilder aus der Festivalstadt.
Bautzen: VEB Domowina-Verlag, 1981. 96 p.: chiefly ill. (some col.)
GT4850.5.B38D78

470

Fünfundsiebzig Erzähler der DDR/ [hrsg. auf der Grundlage der von
Richard Christ und Manfred Wolter besorgten Anthologie ''Fünfzig
Erzähler der DDR'']. Berlin; Weimar: Aufbau-Verlag, 1981. v. 1
PT3740.F78 Bd. 1

471

Hartmann-Laugs, Petra S., 1946– Unterhaltung und Politik im Abend-
programm des DDR-Fernsehens. Köln, Verlag Wissenschaft und
Politik, 1982. 239 p.: ill.   PN1992.6.H37 1982
(Bibliothek Wissenschaft und Politik; Bd. 29)
Bibliography: p. 181–188.

472

Jäger, M. (Manfred) Kultur und Politik in der DDR: ein historischer Abriss. Köln: Edition Deutschland Archiv, 1982. ii, 204 p.

DD261.J29 1982

Includes index.

Bibliography: p. 184–198.

473

Klein, Margrete Siebert. The challenge of communist education: a look at the German Democratic Republic. Boulder [Colo.]: East European Monographs; New York: distributed by Columbia University Press, 1980. xv, 174 p., 7 leaves of plates: ill. LA772.K545

(East European monographs; no. 70)

Includes index.

Bibliography: p. 146–150.

474

Kühnst, Peter, 1946– Der missbrauchte Sport: die politische Instrumentalisierung des Sports in der SBZ und DDR 1945–1957. Köln: Verlag Wissenschaft und Politik, 1982. 210 p.: ill. GV706.8.K84 1982

Originally presented as the author's thesis (doctoral)—Deutsche Sporthochschule Köln.

Includes index.

Bibliography: p. 183–204.

475

Kunsthandwerk aus der DDR: Textilgestaltung, Holzgestaltung: eine Ausstellung des Staatlichen Kunsthandels der DDR im Städtischen Museum Göttingen, 25. September bis 13. November 1983. Göttingen, Das Museum, 1983. 99 p.: ill. NK8850.6.A1K86 1983

476

Die Literatur der DDR/ herausgegeben von Hans-Jürgen Schmitt. München, C. Hanser, 1983. 588 p. PT85.H33 Bd. 11

(Hansers Sozialgeschichte der deutschen Literatur vom 16. Jahrhundert bis zur Gegenwart; Bd. 11)

Includes index.

Bibliography: p. 509–529.

477

Literatur der DDR in den siebziger Jahren/ herausgegeben von P. U. Hohendahl und P. Herminghouse. Frankfurt am Main, Suhrkamp, 1983. 293 p. PT3705.L58 1983

Includes bibliographical references.

CONTENTS: Theorie und Praxis des Erbens/ Peter Uwe Hohendahl
— Kultur und Öffentlichkeit in der DDR/ David Bathrik —
Kunstbewusstsein und geistige Strenge/ Ursula Heukenkamp — Das
Drama der DDR in den siebziger Jahren/ Ulrich Profitlich — Der
verlorene Faden/ Wolfgang Emmerich — Trauer, Tropen und Phan-
tasmen/ Rainer Nägele — "Nun ja! Das nächste Leben geht aber heute
an" / Sara Lennox — Vergangenheit als Problem der Gegenwart/
Patricia Herminghouse.

478

Meissner Porzellan von 1710 bis zur Gegenwart: Österreichisches
Museum für Angewandte Kunst. 24. November 1982 bis 30. April
1983. Wien, Bundesministerium für Wissenschaft und Forschung,
1982. 262 p.: ill.   NK4380.M48 1982
Includes bibliographical references.

479

New Hampshire Symposium on the German Democratic Republic (9th:
1983: World Fellowship Center) Studies in GDR culture and society
4: selected papers from the Ninth New Hampshire Symposium on the
German Democratic Republic. Lanham, University Press of America.
1984.   DD287.3.N48 1983
Includes bibliographical references.

480

Renz, Peter. Sprach- und Literaturwissenschaft in der Bundesrepublik
Deutschland und in der DDR. Erlangen: Institut für Gesellschaft und
Wissenschaft, 1981. 115 p. (ABG: Analysen und Berichte aus
Gesellschaft und Wissenschaft, 5/1981)   H5.A14 1981, no. 5
Bibliography: p. 113–115.

481

Schmidt, Gerlind. Hochschulen in der DDR: eine Untersuchung zum
Verhältnis von Bildungs- und Beschäftigungssystem. Köln: In Kommission bei Böhlau, 1982. 297 p. (Studien und Dokumentationen zur
vergleichenden Bildungsforschung; Bd. 15/4)   LA774.S35 1982
Includes bibliographical references.

482

Sobiella, Jörg. The 150th anniversary of Goethe's death. Dresden: Zeit
im Bild, 1982. 62 p.: chiefly ill. (some col.)   PT2130.W3S6 1982

483

Thomas, Karin, 1941- Die Malerei in der DDR, 1949-1979. Köln: Du-
Mont, 1980. 235 p.: ill.   ND589.T46
   Includes index.
   Bibliography: p. 187-190.

484

Walter, Hans-Albert. Deutsche Exilliteratur 1933-1950. Stuttgart: J. B.
Metzler, 1978-1984. v. 2, 4.   PT405.W24 1978
   Revised enlargement of the ed. published by Luchterhand, Darm-
stadt. Includes bibliographical references and indexes.
   CONTENTS: Bd. 2. Europäisches Appeasement und überseeische
Asylpraxis. — Bd. 4. Exilpresse.

Politics and Government

485

Agsten, Rudolf. Zur Geschichte der LDPD 1949-1952/ herausgegeben
   vom Sekretariat des Zentralvorstandes der Liberal-Demokratischen
   Partei Deutschlands. Berlin, Der Morgen, 1982. 2 v.: ill. (Schriften
   der LDPD; Heft 23)   JN3971.5.A98
   Includes bibliographical references and index.

486

Arndt, Werner. Ostpreussen, Westpreussen, Pommern, Schlesien,
   Sudetenland 1944/1945: die Bild-Dokumentation der Flucht und Ver-
   treibung aus den deutschen Ostgebieten. Friedberg: Podzun-Pallas-
   Verlag, 1981? 208 p.: ill.   D809.G3A84

487

Aussenpolitik der DDR: sozialistische deutsche Friedenspolitik/
   herausgegeben vom Institut für Internationale Beziehungen. Potsdam-
   Babelsberg; Autorenkollektiv unter Leitung von Stefan Doernberg. 2.,
   überarbeitete und erg. Aufl. Berlin, Staatsverlag der Deutschen
   Demokratischen Republik. 1982. 335 p.   JX1549.75 1982
   Includes bibliographical references.

488

Berlin translokal/ Herausgeber, Deutsche Gesellschaft für die Vereinten
   Nationen. Landesverband Berlin. Berlin, Berlin Verlag, 1983. 246 p.
   (Politische Dokumente; Bd. 7)   DD860.B527 1983
   Includes bibliographical references and index.

489

Bichler, Hans, 1945– Landwirtschaft in der DDR: Agrarpolitik, Betriebe, Produktionsgrundlagen und Leistungen. 2., völlig neu bearbeitete Aufl. Berlin: Holzapfel, 1981. 159 p.: ill.   HD1960.5.B52 1981
Includes bibliographical references.

490

Bilaterales Symposium von Historikern der DDR und der Republik Österreich (lst: 1980: Karl-Marx-Universität Leipzig) Internationale Stellung und internationale Beziehungen der deutschen Sozialdemokratie 1871–1900, unter besonderer Berücksichtigung ihrer Zusammenarbeit mit der österreichischen Arbeiterbewegung: Protokoll des 1. Bilateralen Symposiums von Historikern der DDR und der Republik Österreich/ veranstaltet von der Sektion Geschichte der Karl-Marx-Universität Leipzig. 28./29. Mai 1980. Leipzig: Karl-Marx-Universität, 1981. 95 p. (Wissenschaftliche Beiträge der Karl-Marx-Universität. Leipzig. Reihe Gesellschaftswissenschaften)
                                        HX273.B558 1980
Includes bibliographical references.

491

Blanke, Burckhard Michael, 1943– Die politisch-ideologische Bildung und Erziehung in der Nationalen Volksarmee: zum Verhältnis von Militär, Partei und Gesellschaft in der DDR. Bonn, s.n., 1975. 389 p.
                                        UA719.3.B58 1975
Notes: Thesis (doctoral)—Rheinische Friedrich-Wilhelms-Universität zu Bonn. Bibliography: p. 341–389.

492

Bölling, Klaus, 1928– Die fernen Nachbarn: Erfahrungen in der DDR. Hamburg, Gruner + Jahr, 1983. 303 p.: ill.   DD287.4.B65 1983
Includes index.

493

Bundesrepublik Deutschland und Deutsche Demokratische Republik: die beiden deutschen Staaten im Vergleich/ Eckard Jesse (Hrsg.) Berlin: Colloquium Verlag, 1980. 415 p.   DD17.B86
Includes bibliographies.

494

Childs, David, 1933–The GDR, Moscow's German ally. London: Boston: G. Allen & Unwin, 1983. xi, 346 p.: ill.
                                        DD261.C457 1983
Includes bibliographical references and indexes.

495

DDR Handbuch/ hrsg. vom Bundesministerium für Innerdt. Beziehungen; wissenschaftl. Leitung, Peter Christian Ludz; 2., völlig überarb. u. erw. Aufl. Köln: Verlag Wissenschaft u. Politik, 1979. xvi, 1280 p.   DD261.D17 1979

496

East Germany, a new German nation under socialism?/ edited by Arthur W. McCardle and A. Bruce Boenau. Lanham, Md., University Press of America, 1984. xx, 364 p.   DD280.6.E18 1984
Includes bibliographical references.

497

Finn, Gerhard. Politischer Strafvollzug in der DDR. Köln: Verlag Wissenschaft und Politik, 1981. 166 p.   HV9680.5.F56 1981
Includes text of the Strafvollzugsgesetz and the Wiedereingliederungsgesetz.
Includes bibliographical references and index.

498

Forster, Thomas Manfred. The East German Army: the second power in the Warsaw Pact. London; Boston: Allen & Unwin, 1980. 310 p., [2] p. of plates: ill. (some col.)   UA719.3.F6613 1980
Translation of: Die NVA: Kernstück der Landesverteidigung der DDR. Includes bibliographical references and index.

499

Germany (Federal Republic, 1949–). Bundesministerium für Innerdeutsche Beziehungen. Zehn Jahre Deutschlandpolitik: die Entwicklung der Beziehungen zwischen der Bundesrepublik Deutschland und der Deutschen Demokratischen Republik 1969–1979: Bericht und Dokumentation. Bonn: Das Bundesministerium, 1980. 456 p.: ill.   JX1549.Z7A2 1980
Includes index.

500

Hitchens, Marilynn Giroux. Germany, Russia, and the Balkans: prelude to the Nazi-Soviet Non-Aggression Pact. Boulder, East European Monographs New York, Distributed by Columbia University Press, 1983. viii, 350 p. (East European monographs; no. 142)
                                                   DR38.3.G3H57 1983
Includes index.

501

Johnson, A. Ross. East European military establishments: the Warsaw Pact Northern Tier. New York: Crane, Russak, 1982. xiii, 182 p.: ill.

UA829.P7J63 1982

Includes bibliographical references and index.

502

Kistler, Helmut. Die Ostpolitik der Bundesrepublik Deutschland, 1966-1973. Bonn, Bundeszentrale für Politische Bildung, 1982. 175 p.

DD258.85.G35K57 1982

Bibliography: p. 174-175.

503

Klump, Brigitte. Freiheit hat keinen Preis: ein deutsch-deutscher Report. München, Herbig, 1981. 351 p.   DD258.85.G35K59 1981
Includes bibliographical references.

504

McCauley, Martin. Power and authority in East Germany: the Socialist Unity Party (SED). London, England: Institute for the Study of Conflict, 1981. 28 p. (Conflict studies, no. 132)

JN3971.5.A98S65 1981a

Includes bibliographical references.

505

Minnerup, Günter, 1949- DDR, vor und hinter der Mauer. Frankfurt/M, ISP-Verlag, 1982. 107 p.   DD283.M56 1982
Includes bibliographical references.

506

Post, Ulrich, 1953- Die Afrikapolitik der DDR. Hamburg: Institut für Afrika-Kunde, 1982. ix, 158 p. (Arbeiten aus dem Institut für Afrika-Kunde; 43)   DT34.7.P67 1982
Summary in English and German.
Bibliography: p. 147-153.

507

Sandford, Gregory W., 1947- From Hitler to Ulbricht; the communist reconstruction of East Germany, 1945-46. Princeton, N. J.: Princeton University Press, 1983. xiv, 313 p.   HX280.5.A6S245 1983
Includes index.
Bibliography: p. 288-305.

508

Scharf, C. Bradley. Politics and change in East Germany: an evaluation of socialist democracy. Boulder, Colo., Westview; London, F. Pinter, 1984. n. p.   JN3971.5.A2S3 1984
Includes index.

509

Schmitt, Karl. Politische Erziehung in der DDR: Ziele, Methoden u. Ergebnisse d. politischen Unterrichts an d. allgemeinbildenden Schulen d. DDR. Paderborn: Schöningh, 1980. 291 p. (Geschichte, Politik: Studien zur Didaktik; Bd. 2)   JA88.G32S35 1980
Originally presented as the author's thesis, Freiburg i. B., 1977.
Bibliography: p. 269-291.

510

Spanger, Hans-Joachim. Die SED und der Sozialdemokratismus: ideologische Abgrenzung in der DDR. Köln: Wissenschaft und Politik, 1982. 255 p. (Bibliothek Wissenschaft und Politik; Bd. 28)
                    JN3971.5.A98S65 1982
Bibliography: p. 244-254.

511

Weidenfeld, Werner. Die Frage nach der Einheit der deutschen Nation. München: G. Olzog, 1981. 154 p.   DD257.4.W36 1981
Includes index.
Bibliography: p. 141-152.

512

Whetten, Lawrence L. Germany East and West: conflicts, collaboration, and confrontation. New York: New York University Press, 1980. xiv, 215 p.   DD259.4.W438 1980
Includes bibliographical references and index.

Religion

513

Christians and churches in the GDR: a report from the GDR. Berlin: Panorama DDR, 1980. 62 p.   BR856.35.H4413 1980
First ed., written by W. Heyl, published in 1975 under title: Christians and churches in the German Democratic Republic.

514

Knauft, Wolfgang. Katholische Kirche in der DDR: Gemeinden in d.

Bewährung 1945–1980. Mainz: Grünewald, 1980. 238 p.
BX1536.2.K6
Includes bibliographical references and index.

515

Luchterhandt, Otto. Die Gegenwartslage der Evangelischen Kirche in
der DDR. Tübingen: J.B.C. Mohr, 1982. viii, 109 p. (Jus eccle-
siasticum, Bd. 28)   BR856.35.L8 1982
Based on 2 lectures delivered by the author at the Weltkongress für
Sowjet- und Osteuropastudien in Garmisch, 1980.
Includes bibliographical references and indexes.

Society

516

Bach, Roland. Jugend: Solidarität. antiimperialistischer Kampf. Berlin:
Dietz, 1983. 219 p.: ill.   HQ796.B24 1983
"Quellenverzeichnis": p. 215–217.

517

Erbe, Günther. Arbeiterklasse und Intelligenz in der DDR: soziale An-
näherung von Produktionsarbeiterschaft und wissenschaftlich-
technischer Intelligenz im Industriebetrieb. Opladen: Westdeutscher
Verlag, 1982. 224 p. (Schriften des Zentralinstituts für
Sozialwissenschaftliche Forschung der Freien Universität Berlin; Bd.
37)   HD8460.5.E72 1982
Includes indexes.
Bibliography: p. 212–220.

518

GDR, ten years UNESCO membership, 1972–1982. Berlin, UNESCO
Commission of the German Democratic Republic, 1982. 67 p. 16 p.
of plates: ill.   AS4.U825G353 1982

519

Die Gesellschaftlichen Organisationen in der DDR: Stellung,
Wirkungsrichtungen u. Zusammenarbeit mit d. sozialistischen Staat/
[Hrsg., Akad. für Staats- u. Rechtswiss. d. DDR, Potsdam-Babelsberg;
Autorenkollektiv, Margarete Bickner . . . et al.]. Berlin: Staatsverlag
der Dt. Demokrat. Republik, 1980. 286 p.   AS175.G47
Includes bibliographical references and index.

520

Junge Leute in der DDR: Meinungen, Informationen, Fragen. Berlin, Panorama DDR, 1982. 80 p. 16 p. of plates: ill.

HQ799.G5J873 1982

521

Lammert, Ule. Zu Problemen des Städtebaus der achtziger Jahre. Berlin, Akademie-Verlag, 1982. 24 p. (Sitzungsberichte der Akademie der Wissenschaften der DDR. Gesellschaftswissenschaften; Jahrg. 1982, Nr. 12/G)   NA9200.6.A1L35 1982
Includes bibliographical references.

522

Militärbibliothek der Deutschen Demokratischen Republik. Die Nationale Volksarmee: Kern der Landesverteidigung der DDR: empfehlende Bibliographie. Dresden, Die Militärbibliothek, 1980. 167 p.: ill.

Z2250.M54 1980

Includes indexes.

523

Scharf, Wilfried, 1945- Nachrichten im Fernsehen der Bundesrepublik Deutschland und der DDR: Objektivität oder Parteilichkeit in der Berichterstattung. Frankfurt am Main: R. G. Fisher, 1981. iv, 222 p.: ill., map.   PN5214.T4S38
Bibliography: p. 210-222.

524

Shaffer, Harry G. Women in the two Germanies: a comparative study of a socialist and a nonsocialist society. New York: Pergamon Press, 1981. xvi, 235 p.   HC1630.5.S52 1981
Includes index.
Bibliography: p. 211-225.

525

VEB Nachwuchs: Jugend in der DDR/ Haase, Reese, Wensierski (Hg.). Originalausg. Reinbek bei Hamburg, Rowohlt Taschenbuch Verlag, 1983. 250 p.: ill.   HQ799.G53V42 1983
Bibliography: p. 249.

526

Willmann, Lothar. Gefechtsbereit!: die Luftstreitkräfte/Luftverteidigung der Nationalen Volksarmee. Berlin. Militärverlag der Deutschen Demokratischen Republik. 1982. 156 p.: chiefly ill. (some col.).

UG635.G32W52 1982

527

Winter, Kurt, 1910- Das Gesundheitswesen in der Deutschen Demokratischen Republik: Bilanz nach 30 Jahren. 2., überarb. Aufl. Berlin: Verlag Volk und Gesundheit, 1980. 223 p.: ill.

RA502.5.W56 1980

Includes bibliographical references.

LIECHTENSTEIN

528

Batliner, Gérard. Zur heutigen Lage des liechtensteinischen Parlaments. Vaduz: Liechtensteinische Akademische Gesellschaft, 1981. 192 p. (Liechtenstein politische Schriften; Heft 9)   JN2283.B37

Bibliography: p. 182-190.

529

Baumstark, Reinhold, 1944- Masterpieces from the Collection of the Princes of Liechtenstein. New York, Hudson Hills Press, trade distribution by Simon & Schuster, 1981. 321 p., 159 leaves of plates: ill. (some col.).   N5280.L52L5213 1981 fol

UNIFORM TITLE: Meisterwerke der Sammlungen des Fürsten von Liechtenstein: Gemälde. English.

Includes bibliographical references and index.

530

Beiträge zur geschichtlichen Entwicklung der politischen Volksrechte des Parlaments und der Gerichtsbarkeit in Liechtenstein: Anhang, Verfassungstexte 1808-1918. Vaduz: Verlag der Liechtensteinischen Akademischen Gesellschaft, 1981. 304 p. (Liechtenstein politische Schriften; Heft 8)   LAW LIECHTEN 7 Beit 1981

Three of the articles are from a series of lectures sponsored by the Liechtensteinische Akademische Gesellschaft.

Includes bibliographies.

531

Clyne, Michael G., 1939- Language and society in the German-speaking countries. Cambridge, Cambridgeshire, New York, Cambridge University Press, 1984.   PF3973.C55 1981

Not yet in LC..

Includes indexes.

532

Evans, Craig, 1949- On foot through Europe: a trail guide to Austria, Switzerland and Liechtenstein. New York, Quill, 1982. xv, 211 p.

GV199.44.A9E9 1982

Includes bibliographical references.

533

Finke, Heinz, 1915- Liechtenstein: d. liebenswürdige Kleinstaat im Herzen Europas. Konstanz, Stadler, 1977. 184 p.: chiefly ill. (some col.).

DB540.5.F5

Text in English, French, or German with legends in English, French, and German.

534

Fürstentum Liechtenstein: 100 Wanderungen: Routenbeschreibungen von 85 Wanderungen im Talgebiet (Rheintalseite) und 15 Bergwanderungen mit Wegskizzen und Bildern/ bearb. von Johann Oehry, . . . et al. Bern, Kümmerly + Frey, cop. 1979. 167 p.: ill., maps. (Wanderbücher: Internationale Reihe; 5)   DB540.5.F78

535

Das Fürstentum Liechtenstein: ein landeskundliches Portrait/ herausgegeben von Wolfgang Müller. Bühl/Baden, Konkordia, 1981. 271 p.: ill., maps. (Veröffentlichung des Alemannischen Instituts Freiburg i. Br.; Nr. 50)   DB886.F87 1981

536

Fürstentum Liechtenstein. English. The principality of Liechtenstein: a documentary handbook/ edited by Walter Kranz. 5th, rev. and enl. ed. Vaduz, Liechtenstein, Press and Information Office of the Govt. of the Principality of Liechtenstein, 1981. 302 p., 10 p. of plates: ill.

DB886.F8713 1981

Translation of: Fürstentum Liechtenstein.
Bibliography: p. 290-302.

537

Gyger, Walter B. Das Fürstentum Liechtenstein und die Europäische Gemeinschaft. Vaduz: Verlag der Liechtensteinischen Akademischen Gesellschaft, 1975. 245 p. (Liechtenstein politische Schriften; Heft 4)

HC241.25.L54G93 1975

Originally presented as the author's thesis, Hochschule für Wirtschafts- und Sozialwissenschaften, St. Gall. Switzerland.
Bibliography: 233-244.

538

Jansen, Norbert, 1943- Nach Amerika! Geschichte der liechtensteinischen
Auswanderung nach den Vereinigten Staaten von Amerika. Vaduz:
Verlag des Historischen Vereins für das Fürstentum Liechtenstein,
1976. 216 p.: ill.   E184.L55J36
Bibliography: p. 214-215.

539

Kohn, Walter S. G. Governments and politics of the German-speaking
countries. Chicago, Nelson-Hall, 1980.   JN3221.K58
Not yet in LC.
Includes index.

540

Marxer, Peter, 1933- Companies and taxes in Liechtenstein. Vaduz,
Liechtenstein Verlag, 1982. 98 p.   LAW

541

Niedermann, Dieter J. Liechtenstein und die Schweiz: eine völkerrecht-
liche Untersuchung. Vaduz: Verlag der Liechtensteinischen
Akademischen Gesellschaft, 1976. 175 p. (Liechtenstein politische
Schriften; Heft 5)   JX1563.Z7L556 1976
Originally presented as the author's thesis, Hochschule für
Wirtschafts- und Sozialwissenschaften, St. Gall, Switzerland.
Bibliography: p. 166-169.

542

Probleme des Kleinstaates gestern und heute: seiner Durchlaucht Fürst
Franz Josef II, von und zu Liechtenstein zum 70. Geburtstag/ [Mario
von Ledebur-Wicheln . . . et al.]. Vaduz: Liechtensteinische
Akademische Gesellschaft, 1976. 219 p. (Liechtenstein politische
Schriften, Heft 6).   JN2279 1976 .P76
Includes bibliographical references.

543

Reclams Kunstführer Schweiz und Liechtenstein: Kunstdenkmäler und
Museen/ von Florens Deuchler. 3., überarb. u. erw. Aufl. Stuttgart,
Reclam, 1979. 948 p.: ill., 2 maps.   NA1341.R4 1979

544

Roeckle, Heidi. Liechtensteinische Bibliographie, 1960-1973. Vaduz,
Liechtensteinische Landesbibliothek, 1979. ix, 278 p.

    Z2820.R63 1979

545

Schlapp, Manfred. This is Liechtenstein: people and places, yesterday and today, monarchy and democracy, citizen and state, culture, art, and sports, economy and society, domestic and foreign policy. Stuttgart. Seewald Pub. Co. 1980. 276 p., 8 leaves of plates: col. ill.

DB886.S3413 1980

546

Wirtschaft des Fürstentums Liechtenstein. English. The economy of the Principality of Liechtenstein/ edited by Walter Kranz. Vaduz, Govt. Press and Information Office of the Principality of Liechtenstein, 1982. 154 p.: ill.   HC300.5.W5713 1982

Translation of: Die Wirtschaft des Fürstentums Liechtenstein.

547

Zellers, Margaret. Switzerland, the inn way. Southport, Conn., Geomedia Productions; Stockbridge, MA, distributed by Berkshire Traveller Press, 1980. xii, 162 p.: ill.   TX910.S9Z44 1980

Covers Switzerland and Liechtenstein.

Includes index.

SWITZERLAND

Bibliographies and Reference Works

548

Aebersold, Hugo. Sachregister zur Bibliographie der schweizerischen Landeskunde: mit einem Verzeichnis aller erschienenen Faszikel der Bibliographie und dem Hinweis auf die bereits bestehenden Einzelregister. Nendeln: KTO Press, 1976. v. 1.   Z2771.A34

Originally presented as the author's Diplomarbeit, Schweizerische Landesbibliothek, Bern, 1972.

549

Coburg, Beatrice von. Switzerland; selected publications about Switzerland written in English; a bibliography. Berne, Swiss National Library, Information Dept., 1972. iii, 58 p.   Z2771.C6

550

Courten, Régis de. Bibliographies et ouvrages de référence suisses, et plus particulièrement suisses romands: essai de bibliographie analytique. Neuchâtel: [Bibliothèque de la ville: Diffusion, Groupe romand de formation professionnelle de l'Association des bibliothécaires suisses], 1982. 60 leaves.   Z2771.C68 1982

551

Records of genealogical value for Switzerland/ the Genealogical Department of the Church of Jesus Christ of Latter-Day Saints. Rev. Salt Lake City, Utah, U. S. (50 E. N. Temple St., Salt Lake City 84150): The Department, 1982. 16 p.: ill.   CS49.R43 1982
   Bibliography: p. 13–16.

552

Suess, Jared H. Handy guide to Swiss genealogical records. Logan, Utah (P. O. Box 368, Logan 84321): Everton Publishers, 1978. 92 p.: ill.
                                                            CS983.S93
   Bibliography: p. 44–46.

553

Wellauer, Maralyn A. Tracing your Swiss roots. Milwaukee: Wellauer, 1979. i, 115 p.: ill.   CS982.W44
   Includes bibliographies.

Description and Travel

554

Baedeker's Switzerland. English translation, James Hogarth. Englewood Cliffs, N. J. Prentice-Hall, 1982? 328 p.: col. ill., maps.
                                                            DQ16.B17 1982
   One folded col. map inserted at end.
   Includes index.

555

Bützer, Hans-Peter. Unterwegs in Schweizer Parks & Gärten: die herrlichsten und interessantesten Parks und Gärten der Schweiz: mit Angaben, wo es was zu sehen gibt. Bern: Kümmerly & Frey, c1980. 96 p.: numerous ill. (some col.)   SB484.S9B83

556

Bunting, James. Switzerland, including Liechtenstein. New York, Hastings House Publishers, 1973. 224 p. illus.   DQ25.B85

557

Egli, Emil. Switzerland: a survey of its land and people. Berne: P. Haupt, c1978. 229 p., [7] leaves of plates (col.): 29 ill.   DQ17.E513
   Translation of Die Schweiz.
   Includes index.

558

Etter, Alfred. 26 Wanderungen zu Burgen, Schlössern und Klöstern in den Kantonen Graubünden, Schaffhausen, St. Gallen, Thurgau und Zürich. Frauenfeld: Huber, c1980. 164 p., [16] p. of plates: ill. (some col.).   DQ19.E87
    Includes index.
    Bibliography: p. 159–161.

559

Grieben, firm, publishers. Schweiz. München: K. Thiemig, 1979. 260 p.: ill., col. maps.   DQ16.G87 1979
    One map in pocket.
    Includes index.

560

Hoorick, Edmond van. Bergseen der Schweiz/ Texte von Maurice Chappaz und Hans Heierli; mit Aufnahmen von Edmond van Hoorick. Frauenfeld: H. Huber, c1979. 112 p.: numerous col. ill., maps.
DQ25.H66

561

Jeanneret, Francois. Switzerland: Alpine country at the heart of Europe. Washington: J. J. Binns, 1979. 248 p., [1] fold. leaf of plates: ill.
DQ19.J413
    Translation of Schweiz.
    Bibliography:p. 248.

562

Kulturführer Schweiz: in Farbe/ [herausgegeben im Auftrag des Migros-Genossenschafts-Bundes von Niklaus Flüeler]. Zürich: Ex Libris Verlag, 1982. 480 p.: col. ill.   N7141.K84 1982

563

Malerische Reisen durch die schöne alte Schweiz/ mit Beiträgen von Peter F. Kopp, Beat Trachsler und Niklaus Flüeler. Zürich: Ex Libris, 1982. 318, [2] p.: ill. (some col.).   N8214.5.S9M34 1982
    Cover title: Malerische Reisen durch die schöne alte Schweiz, 1750–1850.
    Bibliography: p. 317–[319].

564

Modern Switzerland/ editor, J. Murray Luck. Palo Alto, Calif.: Society for the Promotion of Science and Scholarship, 1978. xvi, 515 p.: ill., map (on lining paper)   DQ17.M63
    Includes bibliographical references and index.

565

Meyer, Werner, 1937– Das grosse Burgenbuch der Schweiz. 2. Aufl.
Zürich: Ex Libris-Verlag, 1978, c1977. 320 p.: ill. (chiefly col.), map
(on lining paper)   DQ19.M58 1978
  Includes index.
  Bibliography: p. 316–317.

566

Powers, Elizabeth, 1944– Switzerland. Tokyo; New York: Kodansha
International, 1978. 137 p.: col. ill.   DQ16.P68

567

Rathgeb, Hans. Ostschweiz: herrliches Land, fleissiges Volk zwischen
Rhein und Alpen. Konstanz: F. Stradler, 1980. 284 p.: ill (some col.).
                                                      DQ57.R18 1980
  Text in English and German; captions in English, French, and
German.

568

Schulthess, Emil. Swiss panorama. Zürich: Artemis, 1982. 203 p.: ill.
(some col.), maps.   DQ19.S287 1982
  Text in English, French, and German.

569

Die Schweiz: eine Annäherung in Bild und Text/ herausgegeben von Max
Mittler. Zürich: Atlantis, 1981. 320 p.: chiefly ill. (some col.).
                                                      DQ26.S38 1981

570

Die Schweiz vom Bau der Alpen bis zur Frage nach der Zukunft: ein
Nachschlagewerk und Lesebuch, das Auskunft gibt über Geographie,
Geschichte, Gegenwart und Zukunft eines Landes. [Zürich]: Migros-
Genossenschafts-Bund, 1975. 703 p.: ill. (some col.).   DQ17.S314

571

Die Schweiz von A-Z: ein Führer durch Feld, Wald und Flur/
[wissenschaftl. Mitarb., Jakob Bill . . . et al.]. Zürich: Verlag Das
Beste aus Reader's Digest, c1979. 502 p.: numerous ill. (chiefly col.),
col. maps.   QH175.S38
  Includes index.

572

Stoll, Victor, 1921– Die 50 Schönsten Wanderungen durch die Schweiz.

Zofingen: Ringier, 1976. 191 p.: chiefly ill. (chiefly coll.).
DQ16.S77
Bibliography: p. 190.

573

Tanner, Alexander. Die römischen Kastelle, Brücken zwischen Kelten und Alemannen: ein Beitrag zu Fragen der Besiedlungskontinuität. Zürich: Historisch-Archäologischer Verlag A. Tanner, 1979. 276 p.: ill.
DQ34.T36 1979
Includes bibliographical references.

574

Zeller, Willy. Über Pässe und Höhen: 56 herrliche Ausflüge. Zürich: Ringier, 1978. 140 p.: numerous ill.   GV199.44.S92A448
Supplements the author's Die schönsten Alpenpässe und Höhenrouten der Schweiz.
Bibliography: p. 138–139.

Economy

575

Eidgenössische Volkszählung 1980: Wohnbevölkerung der Gemeinden, 1900–1980/ Bundesamt für Statistik = Recensement fédéral de la population 1980: population résidante des communes, 1900–1980/ Office fédéral de la statistique. Bern: Das Bundesamt, 1981. v. 1.
HA1594 1980 v. 1
(Statistische Quellenwerke der Schweiz; Heft 701– = Statistiques de la Suisse; 701e– fasc.)
French and German.
Chiefly tables.

576

Frey, René Leo. Wirtschaft, Staat und Wohlfahrt: eine Einführung in die Nationalökonomie. 3., neubearb. und erw. Aufl. Basel [etc.]: Helbing & Lichtenhahn, c1981. 195 p.: 26 ill. (Recht und Wirtschaft aktuell).
HB175.F659 1981
Includes index.
Bibliography: p. 192–193.

577

Gesellschaft zur Förderung der Schweizerischen Wirtschaft. Zahlenspiegel

94

der Schweiz. Zürich: Die Gesellschaft, 1978. 73 p.

HA1605.G47 1978

Tables.

Includes bibliographical references and index.

578

Kanton Bern (n.G.), Volkszählung vom 2. Dez. 1980; Wohnbevölkerung der Gemeinden = Canton de Berne (n.f.), recensement de la population du 2 déc. 1980: population résidante des communes. Bern: Amt für Statistik des Kantons Bern: Kommissionsverlag Stauffacher, 1981. 36 p.   HA1608.B4K36 1981

(Beiträge zur Statistik des Kantons Bern. Bevölkerungsstatistik (Reihe A); Heft 11).

French and German.

579

Made in Switzerland: synopsis of the Swiss export industry. Zürich: A. Vetter, 1976. 325 p.: numerous ill. (some col.)   HC397.M23

580

Margairaz, André. The taxation of corporations in Switzerland: profit and capital taxes of the confederation, cantons, and municipalities. Boston: Kluwer Law and Taxation Publishers, 1983. ix, 139 p.: ill.

HD2753.S9M2913 1983

581

Müller, Bruno, lic. oec. publ. Portfolio und Dynamik in makroökonomischen Modellen: Analysen für kleine offene Volkswirtschaften unter besonderer Berücksichtigung schweizerischer Verhältnisse. Frankfurt/Main: Haag + Herchen, 1981. 116 p.

HB141.M84 1981

(Schriftenreihe des Institutes für Empirische Wirtschaftsforschung der Universität Zürich; Bd. 4)

Originally presented as the author's thesis (doctoral)—Zürich.

Bibliography: p. 116.

582

Oechslin, Roger. Analyse regionaler Disparitäten: Aufbau eines Indikatorenkataloges zur Erfassung der regionalpolitischen Problemlage in der Schweiz. Zürich: Schulthess Polygraphischer Verlag, 1981. xi, 396 p.: ill.   HC397.O34 1981

(Struktur- und regionalwirtschaftliche Studien; Bd. 9).

Originally presented as the author's thesis (doctoral—Hochschule St. Gallen für Wirtschafts- und Sozialwissenschaften)

Bibliography: p. 375-389.

583

Solinski, Helmut A. Volkswirtschaftliche Grundlagen zur Unternehmungsführung im Baugewerbe. Dietikon: Baufachverlag Zürich, 1981.
127 p.: ill.   HB175.S74 1981
Bibliography: p. 126–127.

584

Stopper, Edwin. Notenbank und Wirtschaft: gesammelte Arbeiten. Bern; Stuttgart: P. Haupt, 1974. 252 p., [1] leaf of plates: port.
                                                HG1526.B27 Bd. 22
(Bankwirtschaftliche Forschungen; Bd. 22).

585

Stucki, Lorenz. Das heimliche Imperium: wie die Schweiz reich wurde. Frauenfeld: Huber, 1981. 354 p., [56] p. of plates,: ill.
                                                HC397.S75 1981
     Includes index.
Bibliography: p. 347–350.

586

Wirtschaft und Gesellschaft im Zeichen der Ungewissheit: eine Herausforderung für Wissenschaft und Praxis/ Adrian Hemmer, Hans Ulrich (Hrsg.). Bern (etc.): P. Haupt, c1980. 84 p.: ill.
                                                HB3730.W55
(Weiterbildungsstufe an der Hochschule St. Gallen für Wirtschafts- und Sozialwissenschaften; Bd. 2)
     Contains papers of a seminar organized by the Hochschule St. Gallen in 1979.
     Includes bibliographical references.

587

Wittmann, Walter, 1935– Wohin treibt die Schweiz?: die Schweiz in den achtziger Jahren: verpasste Chancen oder Bewältigung der Zukunft: ein politisch-wirtschaftlich-gesellschaftlicher Schweizer Spiegel. Bern [etc.]: Scherz, 1979. 262 p.   HC396.W57
     Includes index.
Bibliography: p. 256–259.

Intellectual and Cultural Life

588

Dées de Sterio, Alexander. Die 24 Nobel-Preise Schweiz. Rorschach:

Nebelspalter-Verlag, 1982. 135 p.: ill., ports.

Bibliography: p. 135.

589

Geschichte der Schweiz und der Schweizer/ Ulrich Im Hof . . . [et al.];
Redaktion, Beatrix Mesmer (deutsche Ausgabe). Basel: Helbing &
Lichtenhahn, 1982. 3 v.; ill.

590

Das Goldene Buch der Schweiz: Geschichte, Wirtschaft, Wissenschaft
und Kunst, Sitten und Bräuche, die Armee, Tourismus, Gaumen-
freuden und Gastlichkeit, die Natur, Sport und Freizeit/ hrsg. von Paul
Keller. Bern: Edition Colibri, c1978. 352 p.: numerous ill. (some col.).

Includes index.

591

Grenzgänge: Literatur aus der Schweiz 1933–45: ein Lesebuch/
herausgegeben von Hans Rudolf Hilty. Zürich: Unionsverlag, 1981.
523 p.: 31 ill.

592

Handbuch der öffentlichen und privaten Kulturforderung/herausgegeben
von der Schweizerischen Arbeitsgemeinschaft Kultureller Stiftungen
und dem Bundesamt für Kulturpflege. Bern: Edition Erpf, 1983. xxxvi,
847 p.

Text in French, German, Italian, and Romansh.

593

Handbuch der Schweizer Geschichte. Zürich, Verlag Berichthaus,
1972–1977. 2 v.

Includes bibliographies.

594

Hiebel, Friedrich, 1903– Goethe und die Schweiz. Dornach:
Philosophisch-Anthroposophischer Verlag, 1982. 71 p.

Includes bibliographical references.

595

Kunstführer durch die Schweiz/ begründet von Hans Jenny. 5., vollstän-
dig neu bearbeitete Aufl./ herausgegeben von der Gesellschaft für
Schweizerische Kunstgeschichte. Wabern: Büchler, 1971–1982. v. 1–3.:

ill., maps.   N7141.K86 1971
   Maps on lining paper.
   Includes index.
   Contents. — 1. Aargau, Appenzell, Glarus, Graubünden, Luzern,
St. Gallen, Schaffhausen, Schwyz, Thurgau, Unterwalden, Uri, Zug,
Zürich — 2. Genf, Neuenburg, Waadt, Wallis, Tessin — Bd. 3. Basel-
Landschaft, Basel-Stadt, Bern, Freiburg, Jura, Solothurn.

596

Loosli, Carl Albert, 1877–1959. Ihr braven Leute nennt euch
Demokraten: Schriften zur Politik, Geschichte, Kunst und Kultur.
Frauenfeld [etc.]: Huber, c1980. 370 p.   DQ17.L66 1980

597

Sidler, Viktor. Wechselwirkungen zwischen Theater und Geschichte.
Untersucht anhand des schweizerischen Theaters vor Beginn der Refor-
mation. Aarau: Keller, 1973. 239 p.   PT3871.S5
   Bibliography: p. 223–239.

598

Siegfried, André, 1875–1959. Switzerland, a democratic way of life.
Westport, Conn.: Hyperion Press, 1979. 223 p.: ill.
                                                 DQ17.S5213 1979
   Translation of La Suisse.
   Includes index.

599

Tripet, Edgar. Cultural policy in Switzerland: the present situation.
Strasbourg: Council of Europe; [New York: sold by Manhattan Pub.
Co.], 1978. 59 p.   DQ36.T74
   Summary of the report of the Federal Committee of Experts for the
study of questions concerning Swiss cultural policy.

600

Verzeichnis & Lexikon der zeitgenössischen Schweizer Künstler = Réper-
toire & encyclopédie des artistes suisses contemporains = Repertorio
& enciclopedia degli artisti svizzeri contemporanei/ [herausgegeben von
Marcel Mounir]. Miege, Suisse: Éditions M. Mounir. 1983– v. l.: ill.
(some col.).   N7152.V47 1983
   French, German, and Italian.

601

Wolgensinger, Michael. Folklore Schweiz: Brauchtum, Feste, Trachten.

Zürich: Orell Füssli, c1979. 390 p.: 356 ill. (all col.)

GR241.W64

English and French legends (12 p.) inserted.
Includes bibliographical references and index.

Politics and Government

602

Brun, Emil. Menschen führen im militärischen Alltag. Frauenfeld: Verlag
Huber, 1982. 199 p. (Gesamtverteidigung und Armee; Bd. 8)

UB210.B67 1982

Includes index.
Bibliography: p. 183-186.

603

Dürrenmatt, Peter, 1904- Sonderfall oder Endstation: die Schweiz im
sozialistischen Zeitalter. Zürich: Flamberg-Verlag, c1979. 218 p.

JN8766 1979 .D83

604

Garliński, Józef. The Swiss corridor: espionage networks in Switzerland
during World War II. London: Dent, 1981. xviii, 222 p., [12] p. of
plates: ill., maps, 1 facsim., ports.   D810.S7G325 1981
Includes index.
Bibliography: p. 209-213.

605

Handbuch der schweizerischen Aussenpolitik/ hrsg. von Alois Riklin,
Hans Haug, Hans Christoph Binswanger unter Mitw. von Franz
Aschinger . . . [et al.]. Bern; Stuttgart: Paul Haupt, 1975. 1052 p.

DQ69.H33

(Schriftenreihe der Schweizerischen Gesellschaft für Aussenpolitik; 2)
French and German.
Includes index.
Bibliography: p. 921-1014.

606

Koller, Werner. Die Demokratie der Schweiz. Aarau; Frankfurt am
Main; Salzburg: Sauerländer, 1981. viii, 172 p.: numerous ill. (some
col.)   JN8766 1981 .K64
Includes index.
Bibliography: p. 168-170.

607

Kurz, Hans Rudolf. Die Schweizer Armee heute: das aktuelle Standard-
werk über die Schweiz in Wehr und Waffen/ hrsg. in Zusarb. mit
berufensten militärischen und zivilen Fachleuten. Auf den neuesten
Stand nachgeführte und erw. 7. Ausg. Thun: Ott, 1976. 491 p.: ill.
(some col.)   UA802.K8 1976

608

Neutralität, eine Alternative?: zur Militär- und Sicherheitspolitik
neutraler Staaten in Europa/ Dieter S. Lutz, Annemarie Grosse-Jütte
(Hrsg.). Baden-Baden: Nomos Verlagsgesellschaft, 1982. 279 p.: ill.
                                                        UA646.N47 1982
(Militär, Rüstung, Sicherheit; Bd. 4)

609

Petitmermet, Roland. Schweizer Uniformen, 1700–1850: die Uniformen
der Truppen der eidgenössischen Orte und Zugewandten von
1700–1798 und der kantonalen Milizen von 1803–1850 = Uniformes
suisses; les uniformes des troupes des confédérés et de leurs alliés de
1700–1798 et des milices cantonales de 1803-1850. Bern: Historischer
Verein des Kantons Bern [c/o Staatsarchiv, 1977] 1976. xx, 573 p.:
col. ill.   UC485.S9P47
In French and German.
Includes indexes.
Bibliography: p. 567–568.

610

Peyer, Hans Conrad, 1922– Verfassungsgeschichte der alten Schweiz.
Zürich: Schulthess Polygraphischer Verlag, 1978. vii, 160 p.
                                                        JN8719.P49
Bibliography: p. 149–160.

611

Rehsche, Guntram. Schweizerische Aussenwirtschaftspolitik und Dritte
Welt: Ziele und Instrumente, Exportförderung kontra Entwicklungs-
politik? Adliswil: Institut für Sozialethik des SEK Entwicklungsstu-
dien, 1977. 73 p.   HF3706.5.R44
(Entwicklungspolitische Diskussionsbeiträge; 8)
Bibliography: p. 71–73.

612

Schwarz, Urs, 1905– The eye of the hurricane: Switzerland in World

War Two. Boulder, Colo.: Westview Press, 1980. xv, 169 p.: ill.

Includes index.
Bibliography: p. 165.

613

Schweizerisches Symposium der Solidarität. Schwarzbuch Schweiz, Dritte
Welt: Fallbeispiele: Entwicklung heisst Befreiung. Redaktion, Richard
Helbling, Ginevra Signer, Rudolf H. Strahm. Basel: Auslieferung
Terre des Hommes, 1981. 48 p.: ill.   HF1413.S38 1981

614

Sieber, Margret, 1950- Die Abhängigkeit der Schweiz von ihrer inter-
nationalen Umwelt: Konzepte und Indikatoren. Frauenfeld: Huber,
1981. 545 p.: ill.   HF1573.S53 1981
(Zürcher Beiträge zur politischen Wissenschaft; Bd. 3)
Originally presented as the author's thesis (doctoral)—Universität
Zürich, 1979.
Bibliography: p. 475-494.

615

Tschäni, Hans. Wer regiert die Schweiz?: eine kritische Untersuchung
über den Einfluss von Lobby und Verbänden in der schweizerischen
Demokratie. Zürich: Orell Füssli, 1983. 199 p.   JN8852.T72 1983
Bibliography: p. 186-188.
Bibliography of the author's works: p. 188.

616

Die Unheimlichen Patrioten: politische Reaktion in der Schweiz: ein
aktuelles Handbuch/ Jürg Frischknecht . . . [et al.]. Zürich: Limmat-
Verlag, c1979. 512 p.: ill.   JC328.3.U53 1979
Includes index.

617

Winkler, Theodor. Kernenergie und Aussenpolitik: die internationalen
Bemühungen um eine Nichtweiterverbreitung von Kernwaffen und die
friedliche Nutzung der Kernenergie in der Schweiz. Berlin: Berlin
Verlag, 1981. 491 p.   HD9698.S82W56
(Studien zur internationalen Sicherheit; Bd. 7)
Includes index.
Bibliography: p. 443-482.

Religion

618

Locher, Gottfried Wilhelm. Zwingli und die schweizerische Reformation. Göttingen: Vandenhoeck & Ruprecht, 1982. 99 p.

BR410.L63 1982

(Die Kirche in ihrer Geschichte; Bd. 3, Lfg. J1)
Bibliography: p. 1-3.

619

Stoecklin, Alfred. Schweizer Katholizismus: eine Geschichte der Jahre
1925-1975: zwischen Ghetto und konziliarer Öffnung. Zürich [etc.]
Benziger, c1978. 359 p., [8] leaves of plates: ill. BX1591.2.S78
Includes index.
Bibliography: p. 350-351.

Society

620

Casparis, John. Swiss family, society and youth culture. Leiden: Brill,
1979. viii, 106 p. (Monographs and theoretical studies in sociology and
authropology in honour of Nels Anderson; publication 17)

HQ654.C37

Includes index.
Bibliography: p. 102-104.

621

Catrina, Werner. Die Rätoromanen zwischen Resignation und Aufbruch.
Zürich: O. Füssli, 1983. 290 p.: ill. PC909.C3 1983
Bibliography: p. 286-290.

622

Cohen Irvine. Swiss defense profile. [Windsor Forest, Eng.: Diplomatist
Associates, 1977. 31 p.: ill. UA800.C58

623

Damals in der Schweiz: Kultur, Geschichte, Volksleben der Schweiz im
Spiegel der frühen Photographie/ mit Texten von Bruno Fritz-
sche . . . [et al.]. Frauenfeld; Stuttgart: Huber, 1980. 334 p.: chiefly
ill. (some col.), ports. DQ19.D35
Includes bibliographical references and index.

624

Frauen in der Schweiz: von den Problemen einer Mehrheit/ bearbeitet
von Regina Wecker. Zug: Klett und Balmer, 1983. 80 p.: ill.

HQ1703.F74 1983

(Materialien zur Geschichte und Politik in der Schweiz)
Includes bibliographical references.

625

Haller, Gret, 1947– Frauen und Männer: Partnerschaft oder Gleichmacherei?: Versorgungsunabhängigkeit für alle. Gümligen: Zytglogge, 1980. 188 p.: ill.   HQ1075.H34 1980

626

Haug, Werner, 1951– Einwanderung, Frauenarbeit, Mutterschaft: Probleme der schweizerischen Bevölkerungsentwicklung und Bevölkerungspolitik, 1945–1976, Bern [etc.]: P. Lang, c1978. 249 p.: 22 graphs; (Europäische Hochschulschriften: Reihe 22, Soziologie; Bd. 33)   HB3623.H38
  Summary also in English, French, and Italian.
  Bibliography: p. 241–249.

627

Innes, William C. Social concern in Calvin's Geneva. Allison Park, Pa.: Pickwick Publications, 1983. 318 p.   HV355.G4I56 1983
  Includes index.
  Bibliography: p. 309–314.

628

Lebensqualität = Qualité de la vie = La qualita della vita/ [Red., Théo Chopard]. Bern: Jahrbuch der NHG: [c/o] Buri-Druck, 1975. 344 p. (Jahrbuch der Neuen Helvetischen Gesellschaft; Jahrg. 46)
                    HN604.L425
  French, German, and Italian.

629

Lüönd, Karl. Wehrhafte Schweiz: die Truppengattungen unserer Armee. Zürich [etc.]: Ringier, [1979]. 144 p.: numerous ill. (some col.)
                    UA800.L83
  Bibliography: p. 144.

630

Macht und ihre Begrenzung im Kleinstaat Schweiz/ herausgegeben von Werner Kägi und Hansjörg Siegenthaler. Zürich; München: Artemis Verlag, 1981. 269 p. (Zürcher Hochschulforum; Bd. 1)
                    HM271.M29
  Includes bibliographical references.

631

Meier, Hans-Peter, 1944– CH-Cement: das Bild der Schweiz im Schweizervolk. Zürich: Eco-Verlag, 1982. 214 p.: ill.
                    HN603.5.M44 1982

632

Mohler, Armin, 1920– Wider die All-Gemeinheiten, oder, Das Besondere ist das Wirkliche. Krefeld: Sinus-Verlag, 1981. 137 p.

HC79.E5M63 1981

Bibliography of the author's works: p. 136–137.

633

Schelbert, Leo. Einführung in die schweizerische Auswanderungsgeschichte der Neuzeit. Zürich: Leemann, 1976. 443 p. (Beihefte der Schweizerischen Zeitschrift für Geschichte; Heft 16)

JV8281.S33

Includes indexes.
Bibliography: p. 352–412.

634

Schmid, Carol L. Conflict and consensus in Switzerland. Berkeley: University of California Press, 1981. vii, 198 p.: ill.

HN603.S35

Includes index.
Bibliography: p. 183–193.

635

Schweizer, Niklaus R. (Niklaus Rudolf), 1939– Hawaii and the German speaking peoples. Honolulu, Hawaii: Topgallant Pub. Co., 1982. xiv, 218 p.: ill.   DU624.5.S38 1982

Includes index.
Bibliography: p. 193–206.

636

Schweizerischer Israelitischer Gemeindebund. Die Jüdische Bevölkerung der Schweiz im Spiegel der Volkszählung 1970/ Schweizerischer Israelitischer Gemeindebund. Zürich: Der Gemeindebund, 1975. 2 v.

DS135.S9S3 1975

637

Switzerland, its people and culture/ Lynn M. Hilton, editor-in-chief. Skokie, IL: National Textbook Co., 1979. 94 p.: ill.

DQ17.S93 1979

638

Wiedmer-Zingg, Lys. Der Preis der Emanzipation. Zürich: Orell Füssli, c1980. 230 p., [12] leaves of plates: ports.   HQ1236.W46

104

639

Die Zukunftstauglichkeit der schweizerischen Entscheidungsstrukturen/
Herausgeber, Andreas Blum, Gerhard Kocher, Walter Wittmann.
Diessenhofen: Rüegger, 1982. 77 p.   JN8766 1982
Includes bibliographical references.

NAME INDEX

(Works not entered under author are listed by title)

108